VAMPIRES TO SUCCESS

A journey of

Accomplishing Your Ideas

And Creating

A Fortune

Vampires to success have encircled Victor; he reaches a capital city to earn a living. The city unveils clandestine concepts which act as an armor to combat the vampires who were sucking the blood out of his ambitions. This war brings a glorious life to Victor.

This book touches you at a deep level and bridges the gaps which keep you away from being exceptional. It challenges present-day philosophies of triumph, and helps to accomplish the goals of life in a new way.

Refreshing experiences and short stories, "A Mango Millionaire", "Small T to Big T", "Cannot Succumb to Fear", "Remain in Shade My Son", "Monk's Mysterious Blessings", "Letter to Mom" thrill and make you ride on an intellectual roller-coaster.

It is a time-honored fact, any formula produces equal results if applied with alike numbers. A gigantic success needs - multiplication of actions, the addition of knowledge, a division of goals (short term and long term) subtraction of excuses and correct values. This book reveals those correct enigmatic values to accomplish definitive outcomes in pursuit of your goals. Any flaw is a vampire and the moment it infects, you turn into a slave. In an average lifespan numerous vampires dupe you and drag into the obscurity.

The book takes an in-depth look at the power of mind and illustrates how these forces influence your success. It helps to discover your foremost potentials and brings finest self-contentment.

This book is bursting with fresh ideas, here are a few great ones:

1. **Making Decisions** – Keys to make sagacious decisions?

2. **The Finest Cut Concept** - How to distinguish your work and yourself, without belittling others?

3. **Only Eight Happiness of The Life** – Which are these and how to proliferate those?

4. **Money, Success, Love, Care** – How can they go hand in hand, without compromises?

5. **Most Sought After People** – How can you be the one?

It captures all essentials to become a productive and intellectual individual; adds fuel to the burning desire of success and acts as a guiding light. By the time you finish reading it, you would have identified all vampires and the ultraviolet rays to kill them. Never in life again you will succumb to weaknesses and always emerge as a conqueror.

The intent is vital to any effort – this book intends to benefit you by deciphering the methods of efficacious people who turn their average lives by three sixty degrees, and if you observe diligently, you find, many such around you. The learnings help you to know, what they do inversely to reach and prevail at the pinnacle of success.

Bearing in mind the fact that, most of the people do not read beyond a few pages after they buy a book, conscientious efforts are made to keep it flavorsome, enjoyable and straightforward. Every chapter is a short and complete message, which offers a sense of accomplishment and you learn from each one.

I thank you for picking 'Vampires to Success.' I assure, if you persistently follow, even a few concepts of the book you would become richer, happier and more successful than ever.

Accolades for Vampires to Success

"A must read, may be the next big thing after 7 habits and Think and Grow Rich!!!" **Goodreads.com**

"I wish I could take this powerful & beautiful book and give it in the hands all young people (who are going to begin their career), lower, middle and senior management professionals." **Amazon.com**

"Great book, very insightful, close to real life, truly depicts the challenges in an office/ business environment and strategies to overcome them!!" **Amazon.com**

"Once I started reading it.. I could not keep it down. Success could not have been better defined." - **Amazon.com**

"The book is different. I have started reading it and am loving it. I have given it a 5-star rating as I have read a lot of self-help books and I can say this book is very useful. – **Amazon UK**

"I have read hundreds of books over the past many years in my quest for success. "Vampires to Success" truly stands right near the top. It has made a positive impact on my life in many ways." **Amazon.in**

"I was surprised by all that I learned by going through the steps in the book. A sure way to handle your success." **– Amazon.in**

"Interesting Book.. A different perspective towards achieving success, worth a read !" **– Amazon.in**

"A very good read." **Amazon Australia**

"This book should be on every bookshelf in every home." **Amazon.in**

ACKNOWLEDGEMENTS

I have been blessed to have an extraordinary combination of people in my life, who help me to excel in the expedition called life.

A huge thanks to my family and friends; without them my voyage would have been worthless. Special thanks to the gifted friends who have played as critique to bring the best in this book.

A colossal thanks to the readers who established Vampires to Success as an eBook wonder before the print version. Without all your support this remarkable achievement was not even imaginable. Thanks for all your amazing reviews that inspire me. Also, thanks to all future readers who want to achieve excellence and make this world a gorgeous place to live.

VJ Cartier

Author

Chapter – 1

"Victor – The Poor, Average, Directionless guy."

The Vampire of Wrong Environment

"I began my career as an economics professor but became frustrated because the economic theories I taught in the classroom didn't have any meaning in the lives of poor people I saw all around me. I decided to turn away from the textbooks and discover the real-life economics of a poor person's existence."

- Muhammad Yunus, Nobel Laureate

From the window of his top-floor apartment in New York, Victor observes grandeur of the city outside, he notices the view is captivating enough to embrace the eyes. The apartment offers him an unobstructed view of the surroundings. Currently, he heads one of the top Multi-National Companies, owns shares in multiple ventures, a few exquisite homes in different countries and a collection of luxury cars. He is a shining star in the community of influential entrepreneurs and CEOs known for the matchless delivery of results. His strong personality and high morals inspire youths and they dream to be like him.

As the breeze ruffles his hair, he thinks about the meaning of his name and whispers – umm…. a person who defeats an opponent in a battle, game, or other competition - victorious.

It is true in his case. He neither belonged to this country nor had he born in a privileged community. Victor, with the nickname 'Vick' belonged to a minuscule suburban village in the Himalayan valleys. He had grown up in an environment with limited material resources. A few new dresses, no toys and rarely bought over-sized shoes had been a daily reality for Victor, and most of the families in the area lived identical.

He had a timid directionless mind, this state of mind often emerged as many vampires to conquer. His inadequacies and feebleness were the vampires, their sharp fangs penetrated deep into his vulnerable mind, and sucked the success quotient out of him. They could have bitten him more and turned him into a perpetual slave, had he given in; however he did not. Instead, he had come across incredible mentors and learned to apply their wisdom to protect himself and excel further.

Victor had not only selfishly protected himself but also defended numerous people, he attacked the vampires with self-devised strategies.

He delighted with the realization that he had never manipulated or exploited anybody to be successful, this spreads a divine calmness on his face.

Till the youth, he had lived a life with limited financial resources— queued for buses, admissions, clinics, hospitals and almost everywhere, waiting for opportunities characterized his life.

It is advantageous to know how people below average means spend their lives, in some countries, the have-nots need to wait enormously at places of worship to see the deities; often priority is given to the wealthy and influential people. Thus, waiting penetrates their lives in every imaginable way.

To buy necessities becomes a project – they save for a couple of years, aspire to buy 'something' and, by the time they are closer to buy 'something,' 'something else' crops up and shatters the dream. They still use prepaid mobiles with a closed fist, spend each penny guardedly and even today, a massive chunk of the population is away from the internet and technology since it remains unaffordable for the most, which in turn, reduces their growth potential.

As a child, Victor had never felt it unusual, he firmly believed this is how life went on for all.

He goes to the flashback when:

A terrible tragedy strike upon Victor and his family, his father, the sole breadwinner of the family dies in an accident, it proves a titanic misfortune for the entire family. He is the youngest of four siblings, studies in his final year of college, and there are a lot of negative and nil positive influences on him. After his father's death, his already strained life becomes tougher. At this stage,

Victor does not take any decision whether to work or to drop his education. He could not think at all.

Groomed in an average humble family, he had no education to handle a crisis. When it appeared, he rarely had any expertise to act on it.

Victor's mother is a lady with limited educational qualifications, she had experienced the harsh realities of life and knows well that now survival will be difficult. She calls Victor and his brother Prince who are almost the same age, for a conversation.

Mother: "Prince and Vick, we will not have the life we have lived so far, and the situation will change now. There will be no support from anywhere, and we need to manage everything on our own."

She adds, "You cannot continue your studies further as the money on hand is hardly enough to make both ends meet."

Victor could not apprehend why his mother's words had such a profound impact on him. Perhaps, his father's death had shocked him and drastically impacted his thinking process, because earlier he never took such discussions seriously.

Conclusive actions from the discussion comes as below:

1. Victor and his brother will have to find work somehow and make a living.

2. There would be no support from others, and they need to find their own means of survival.

Most people face this situation at some stage in different contexts of their lives. Victor's life is no different; he is an average person surrounded by the vampires.

In advance to the exams results of the final year, he packs his two pairs of clothes and with no significant ambitions, leaves for the capital city- the mega city which had served as a platform for various entrepreneurs. The city will expose him to different challenges and, to the concepts which will force him into the direction of remarkable success.

After eighteen hours of travel, he touches the city, it is the first time he sees such a colossal city with skyscrapers, too many vehicles, and people. He jokingly tells himself that the city is good for anyone to get lost. His mother had spoken to a relative, to help him find accommodation, and the person comes there to receive him. He takes Victor to a place which is exceptionally mobbed, congested and dirty with dearth popping out from its all possible corners— it becomes his journey's origin point.

We face vampire of the erroneous environment; it can be at our home, school or office. When we are young, we are unaware and feeble to face it, but once we are grown up and enlightened, we must acquire skills, courage and make conscious efforts to enter into a war and defeat this vampire. Mythology and history have numerous incidences of good winning over the evil, but they emerged victorious only after the best fight put forth, like that we must start a full-fledged war against these flaws which attack us in many forms, and we must change the environment around or move out of it to succeed.

Chapter – 2

God's Angel and Ultraviolet Ammunition of "Integrity within Yourself."

The Vampire of Disintegrity

"For he will command his angels concerning you to guard you in all your ways" - Bible

Victor spends two months in search of work, he notices the city is not benevolent enough to provide stress-free opportunity. Placement agents are interested in finishing registrations and charge fees rather than find real jobs. Companies which place notices on hoardings look for the references, no one is ready to trust a new person like him. The hope almost dies, but he had no other option.

When you have no options, the best strategy is to stay there, even if you are happy or sad, encouraged or depressed, painful or relaxed, until the time you get what you want. Mostly, you succeed in life if there is no one to fall back upon and you acknowledge this fact but still do not give up, the pleasures which follow after all you undergo are immense.

Victor sits in the congested stinky compound and thinks about his future, he prays for the circumstances to change, somehow. He desperately wants to do something. One day he views a person, he notices that he wore expensive clothes and wristwatch. Victor had seen this person there a couple of times, and he feels nice about him even without any acquaintance. With all hopes, he thinks to speak to the person and inches towards him.

"Hi! I am Vick" He gathers all his courage and introduces himself. The person looks at Victor, from head to toe as if he is evaluating him through some analytical instrument. It flashes in Victor's mind that God has sent an angel to help him and immediately, his brain starts a conversation, "I can be wrong .To any person in need, the people who might help seem like an angel," "But maybe I am correct, something happens for the first time somewhere."

"Hi Vick, I am Patrick, people call me Pat." They chat, and after that Patrick goes, he appears a busy person. Victor judges him as successful and wonders that why he stays in such area when he can easily afford a nice place to live. However, his current focus is to get some work with his help, so he disengages from the thought.

For next one week, he does not encounter Patrick. "Has the angel disappeared?" the ray of hope he had glimpsed in Patrick was darkening. Victor feels lost again. He does not know Patrick's home address to inquire. The week passes after week; there is no sign of Patrick even after two weeks.

"Always know the sources, where you can get help from and more importantly, ask for it when you need."

He continues with his directionless, halfhearted efforts, visits the companies, agents, reads employment newspapers, advertisement, and does everything in his purview. The situation disheartens him, and his efforts bear no fruits. It is dark all around for Victor, "Only You can save me now, do You listen to me?" he pleads God.

After two and a half weeks Victor hears a voice, his heart pounds fast.

"Hey, Vick! How are you doing, did you find any work?"

Victor is unable to believe that Patrick is in front of him, it culminates in a state of silence. The angel has appeared again resurrecting hopes.

"Is everything alright?" re-questions Patrick.

Back from the state of shock, Victor replies: "Nothing is OK Pat, only one positive sign, I met you again." He tells Patrick about his story, in brief, his family conditions and the incident which has compelled him to come to the city.

"Okay" encourages Patrick "In our life, we always need to tell the exact position to get a realistic solution." He continues, "Though I understand that you are in trouble of being unemployed, is there any other cause which bothers you, my friend?"

"Nothing else Pat, it is the only reason which worries me all the time, I am not sure whether I would ever be of any value to my family. I need one chance to prove myself, I promise to put all efforts to do an excellent job which will make everyone happy."

Patrick's calm and deep eyes fix on Victor's face, he looks in his eyes and feels his pain. He observes that Victor's request is honest, and he would do what he had expressed a few moments ago. He epilogs,

"There are many needy people around me, and I cannot help all of them. But I think, I can help this one who seems to be in agony and looks sincere."

Patrick is a young man in his early thirties. He asserts to himself "Let me try to help him with a few concepts which may give his life a direction."

Patrick states "Vick, I can help you, but I may not vouch for you because you are needy and I am benevolent, you need to deserve a commendation. I can give you some time and share the lessons I have learned in life."

"I will tell you about a few ideas in coming days, which may help you to accomplish your dreams."

Victor feels fantastic to hear these words, he is prepared to do whatever it takes to succeed in life, and no one had spoken to him like this so far. They decide to meet daily to begin the learnings – morning or evening dependent on Patrick's availability.

"Think about this Vick – How were we created, why were we created that way? I will reveal my thoughts on that when we meet next."

Victor feels it as the most difficult question thrown on him in entire life, scientific, philosophical or biological, what can be the answer? Victor ponders over all possibilities but cannot find one which precisely meets his view.

He says "I will check with Pat when we meet." That night he goes to bed peacefully, hopeful for a good future.

Patrick had advised him to meet in the Joggers Park, next day. When Victor reaches there, the sun spreads his golden light, and the dew on the jade grass shines. He waits for Patrick, who appears exactly at 6 AM, from behind a lush green hedge, in his pure white tracksuit he resembles an angel.

"He has a remarkable personality" Victor monologues.

After greetings, the conversation begins, "So, do you remember the question I asked, have you thought about it?"

"Yes Pat, how were we created, why were we created that way?"

"Hmm that is wonderful, so what is the answer?"

Victor continues "I looked into several aspects, and each time, my mind ran in a different direction, one thought opposing other, one point countering another, I am sorry I could not decide what can be the answer to this question. I am eager to know it from you."

Patrick understands that the vampire of dis-integrity has bitten Victor, he senses that this vampire can be killed only by the ultraviolet ammunition of 'Integrity within Yourself.'

He asks, "Have you ever tried to interpret, what can be the purpose of same?"

Victor: "Honestly, I never thought about it Pat, until you asked me."

Patrick: I know, you have not solved the riddle, but the thoughts you expressed have all the answers hidden. I will help you to learn how to seize those answers from your thoughts for any question.

Victor: Is this possible Pat? This idea is a stranger to me. If my words have the answer in it, how can you see those and I cannot? Is there some different vision which provides you an answer? Patrick sits on a bench and initiates,

"Sit comfortably, and let me explain what I see and you do not see.

There is a definite purpose behind each creation, whether it is by God, nature or humans. Purpose gives us a strong rationale for why we do, what we do and makes us stick till achievement. Each creation is designed to reach its maximum potential and to find the reason for our existence is our prime responsibility.

God creates us in an integrated form with all required parts to make us successful in one place, whether it is the brain, heart or limbs everything integrates into one body. He does not create us in dispersed form with an option to carry a few organs at a time and leave others behind, each creation is one integrated unit. This anatomy is easy to understand, correct?"

Victor inquires, "Yes, I get that Pat, our body is always integrated, and wherever we go, it moves together, it is a simple fact and I am aware of it like all others. So, with due regard I register that I cannot comprehend, how do we disintegrate? I do not get what you mean by this?"

Patrick: "This is a basic but an excellent question Vick, and this is how I also thought earlier, the vampire is not 'unawareness', with the Internet and all new age learning resources, the info is abundant, 'We are aware of everything' is the new problem.

The vampire strikes when we need to implement the facts we already know. The current challenge is, how to prioritize a few concepts from the endless knowledge and apply what benefits us to get better results and become more successful. At the conceptual crossroads, the vampire looks and grins as he knows you are in a trap, and bites.

My aim is to remind you, if you recognize the purpose you can achieve the maximum potential. As Samuel

Johnson, the famous English writer once mentioned, *"People need to be reminded more often than they need to be instructed."*

Victor: "That sounds fascinating Pat, please tell me more, how can I become more deserving than needy, I feel that I am going to learn a significant lesson today."

Pat continues "That's phenomenal Vick, you make progress when you take an interest.

Another top notch visionary, Albert Einstein once remarked, "Imagination is more important than knowledge. Knowledge is limited. Imagination encircles the world."

So, let us push the pedals of our imaginations and proceed. The limitation of education is that it can make you read but, it cannot force you to learn against your wish, and there is a mammoth difference in reading and learning.

Education tells you what has happened in the past but, it fails to show you what the possibilities are. Though knowledge is unlimited, the benefits and applications are very limited. You need to learn how to apply what benefits you." Patrick stops for a moment.

Victor had never entered into such a discussion in the past, Patrick's message gets direct to his brain, and he tries to connect the dots to see the larger picture of life. Although he knew a few things broadly, he had never looked at life from this point of view.

Patrick continues "Have you ever imagined the engine of a car pulling it into two directions? A hypothetical situation, but that's why imagination is resilient than knowledge; it would be called malfunctioning, and immediately, we will send the car to a workshop. For machines, it is easier to identify the problem which makes them dysfunctional, there is technical know-how available to determine the errors and workshops effortlessly rectify those.

We humans are not like that, our engine, the brain pulls us into multiple directions, others cannot diagnose it, and more threatening is the fact that most times we ourselves fail to recognize this.

This situation is a dilemma and to succeed, we need to end this. Mental unification is the first step of the journey which leads to accomplishments."

Patrick stops and questions, "Now you know, why you were not able to see the answer even when all thoughts were present in your mind?"

"Yes Pat, I can now correlate, I had varied thoughts in my mind, which pulled my brain in different directions."

Patrick: Yes, this is natural, remember that the only person who can take you out of this dilemma is you. You need to use your wisdom in such a manner that you do not get lost in the maze of counter opinions. These crisscrosses force you to lose your way; you do not reach your destination. Instead of this confusion, you need the unifying forces of your brain to unfold the answers and help you to move in the direction of success.

Back to the point, when God created us, the creation was meant to be used as one. However, when you got delivered in this unified form, you had the world around you to teach, what is right and wrong, what can be done, cannot be done. There might have been motivating people around, who motivated and set the unrealistic expectations, thus building undue pressure on you and also there might be demotivating people around, who added to the pressure with their strong belief that you are worthless. It depends on the environment where you have grown up.

All these people are around us throughout life, and they can be anyone, you would know it better.

With no malice, they all wanted you to be successful in their own fashion. When you grew up around all those people, you got 'conditioned' in a certain way, which means a state in which you live for years, and it creates a significant influence in the way you think and visualize all situations. It creates your self-image. It concerns that you do not realize the fact that this image is an outcome of external factors around you. To observe it, pay attention to the way people in a particular society speak, dress, walk and eat. Honestly, there is no 'self' in this self-image.

If you can change your perception, you can change your emotions, and this leads to a new beginning. It is paramount to create your image which thoughtfully considers the external environment but is not much influenced by it, your self-image needs to be a product of your own thoughts and actions.

Vick, the environment in which you have grown up was contradictory, for most people, it's like that. Two people with different opinions influence you, on the same situation and you know, everyone always has an opinion, whether they know about the subject or not, if you go to them you are sure to get an advice.

As a commoner, we choose opinion not by virtue of it, but by the value of a relationship with the individual who has given it. When we have doubt in an opinion, we go to the next person who is more likely to agree with our line of thinking.

While growing up, you always got multiple opinions on any subject, that's why given any situation; your brain sprints in various directions, and you are not able to conclude what is the right action under this scenario. Your mind consistently diverts you in different directions which generate a state of indecisiveness and ultimately leads to ineffectiveness. Today, the entire world is looking for accuracy at the speed of light, but the outcome of such delays translates to a mediocre performance and a substandard life.

Patrick continues, "I am sure Vick, like most people you do not want to live an ordinary life and the purpose of your life is way bigger. To achieve this, you need to live as an integrated being – your mind, body, and soul, all at one place. The journey of success in life begins with 'integrate within'. Once you do that, you start moving in one direction, which is crucial to achieve any goal. You need to cut all strings and break all barriers which make you disintegrated. Do you comprehend this?"

"Yes I do understand Pat, I need to integrate myself from within, create my own image, and I need to apply the power of integrity which will help me to get the right answers. I realize why God has created me this way and how to take maximum advantage of it. I thank you for providing me a new perspective to look at the things. Also, I do realize the importance of purpose which keeps us driving throughout life, if I detach from the purpose I end up losing interest in my work. The purpose is an anchor which helps us to stick to the goals." affirms Victor.

Patrick praises, "You figured it out, Vick. The biggest risk of all risks is indecisiveness. Because of not having integrity within most people are not able to make a lot of important decisions and later regret the loss of opportunity where they could have done something which could have altered their lives for better.

If you have understood this point, we will move to the next learning. We need to expose the vampires of fear which hold us back from making decisions. How does that sound?"

Victor states, "Sure, I have a keen interest to learn about the fears which impact our decision making. I promise that I will apply the concept of 'Integrity within Yourself' and give my synchronized efforts for any objective I undertake.

Patrick: OK, let's meet here again tomorrow, same time. I assume you will rethink about the point which we have discussed today.

Today when Victor reminisces the concept he appreciates the immense value it has delivered to him. He has killed the vampire of dis-integrity with ultraviolet ammunition of 'Integrity within Yourself'.

"When you integrate within, you turn on the wheels of the chariot to fortune." He whispers.

"My life turned when I realized I had to take responsibility for what was happening in my life. To stop blaming other people and situations, and to start taking meaningful action."

– Benny Hsu

Chapter – 3

"Hammer of Integrity"

The Vampires of Fear

"You gain strength, courage, and confidence by every experience in which you stop to look fear in the face. You must do the thing which you think you cannot do." -

Eleanor Roosevelt

Next day when Victor reaches the park he finds Patrick already meditating there. No wonders! He always looks radiant. Exactly at six AM, the alarm of Patrick's wristwatch rings, and he opens his eyes.

Victor is about twenty steps away from him.

"Good morning Vick, Today I came slightly early to have a word with God. I feel that when we meditate He speaks to us, and when we pray He listens to us."

Victor wishes, "Good morning Pat! You have a deep faith in God, would you define what faith is for you?"

Pat: "In my view, faith is consistent, which remains unaffected during ups and downs of life, which keeps guiding you even in dark and turbulent times, faith is eternal. I am a firm believer and thus is my faith.

My faith does not link only with one aspect; it is present in all extrinsic and intrinsic values. Without faith, you can achieve nothing.

We get up each morning having faith that sun will rise, and fresh water will be there. Faith that our loved ones will be well and flourish. Faith that the Mother Earth will continue to fulfill our needs. Faith that air we breathe will be full of oxygen. We casually take faith for granted, but unknowingly, we always demonstrate strong faith. Faith is the power which makes entrepreneurs produce anticipated products, with a strong self-assurance that people would buy their products. The belief that their organization will help people to earn more than bread and butter, and enable them to live a prosperous life. Investors invest because they have faith that their money will grow.

If you have faith you produce faith, it impacts everyone very positively. It is my vision, and you may have your own."

Ok, so let us start now from where we left yesterday, did you revisit the learning and do you want me to clarify something?"

"No Pat, all clear that was the best session I ever had, I am enthused to know about the 'Vampires of Fear," exclaims Victor.

"That's really nice! Today, I will glide you through vampires of fear, they are many and impact decision making. Prior to that here is a real-world experience:

"Cannot Succumb to Fear."

In 2016, The US President Barack Obama on one Monday requested Americans not to surrender to terror after manifold, new attacks in New York City and New Jersey., vowing to combat the self-professed Islamic State terrorist group out of the country and its dogma at home.

Obama declared ""They are trying to hurt innocent people, but they are also trying to inspire fear in all of us. We all have a role to play as citizens in making sure we don't succumb to that fear."

Americans are under tremendous threat of terrorism, and the President who represents them exhibits a strong courage, he is fighting with the vampires to humanity; entire nation does not succumb to fear, and that is why they are the most powerful country in the world. This approach had solidified when The US Navy Seals executed Osama Bin Laden in Abbottabad, Pakistan, once the deadliest terrorist of the world; brought to justice.

You must treat the vampires of fear the same way – identify, find, combat, and terminate it. Otherwise, they continue to attack, and you remain a prey.

These are the six vampires of fear which hold us from decision-making, let us start with the first one:

1. Vampire of Making Mistakes:

Most people do not decide as they are afraid of making mistakes, they are scared of getting the things wrong at the first attempt. They forget that mistakes are also the stepping stones of success. There are some risks associated with any decision, but the bigger risk is not to take any risk. We lose a lot of opportunities because we do not take the chance, we surrender even without trying. I encourage you to take your chances.

Let me share a story,

"Small T to a Big T."

This story is a true life experience of a minuscule tea stall owner who, with his risk taking ability takes his life to an entirely different level.

There was a person, who had a very insignificant tea-stall near a seaport, this tea stall was the small 'T'. His customers were mostly, the truck drivers who used to carry loads from the seaport to various cities. On the way, they used to have a cup of tea on his roadside tea stall. During that time the drivers used to discuss the cost of operations including fuel, driver, consumables, operating cost, total revenue and profits which the owners made.

The Tea-Vendor was neither educated nor raised in a business environment. However, he was wise and capable of evaluating the benefits of operating as a transporter. He was a motivated risk taker for sure. He gave it a go.

He put everything on stake, his land, wife's jewelry and the tea-stall. He invested all his money in buying a truck, this became the big 'T'. It was an enormous risk for a person of his capacity. What if the things did not work out the way he had imagined? But he was determined to change his pity life.

It's not that people did not advise him, not to do so. Still, he went ahead with his decision and today, he owns a fleet of more than three hundred trailers catering to the transportation requirements of top companies in the northern region of the country. He never had to look back, he succeeded because he was not afraid to take his chances, own mistakes and embrace the consequences of his deeds.

Now, when people ask him, he says, "I still deal in T, it's just that, now I focus on a bigger T."

2. Vampire of Failures:

The latest quandary in our environment is too much focus on success, no one applauds failures, and that is good in a way. Conversely, failure is not bad, as it can teach you a lot and those experiences further help you to rectify the path of success. Do not worry if people laugh at you when you try something new and fail in initial efforts. As a norm, most people do not find new actions worth trying. These new goals are unconventional and do not exist in routine life.

To signify this Mahatma Gandhi the Great Indian Leader of independence commented, "First they ignore you, then they laugh at you, then they fight you, then you win." He used this experiment to free his nation, and it was totally unimaginable at those times. No one had got independence through nonviolence so far.

If the legendary inventors had been afraid of failures, there would have been no "Air-craft" "Light-Bulb" and "Radium."

The Wright Brothers fearlessly dreamt and invented an aircraft. In Orville's own words "We were lucky enough to grow up in an environment where there was always much encouragement to children to pursue intellectual interests; to investigate whatever aroused curiosity." Today most of the world is connected by the fearless dream of Wright Brothers.

Never be afraid of failures, think and act fearlessly.

3. <u>**Vampire to Thinking Bold:**</u>

If we grow in an environment of tame thinkers, who spent their lives making both ends meet, we would be like any other average person on this planet.

The solution is to self-learn and intensify thoughts to avoid these influences. You might have come across notions like "Success is not easy," "When you earn, then you will come to know; how difficult it is to make a living," "Money does not grow on trees."

Vick, at least I came across all these prior to I started earning.

People share their experiences when they open their mouths. But it's not necessary that their experience becomes your experience too. You can definitely have a different mindset. You can have different experiences and different outcomes. There would be many successful people around you as well, notice them. Do not hesitate, stay around them, and ask them about the things you want to learn, ask for guidance, and ask about the actions they took to reach this stature.

Even if they are not open to share, you can still learn through observation — observe how they think on a particular subject, which solution they come up with, what they suggest, and how they execute. Watch and follow those with intense focus.

Use all your senses and convert to an avid learner. A few sources to learn are books, mistakes, failures, other's success, failures, and experiences. Attend the classes you need, also absorb from TV, internet, podcasts and Movies. Today even illiterates can learn, it is so convenient for all.

I am sure Vick, you would add to the list as you move forward in life.

Never choose a non-achiever to be your mentor, learn from achievers as that will be a critical factor to create a fortune.

4. Vampire of Solitude:

Human beings are social animals. Being a social animal, we have the tendency to live in herds, we want to be around the acquaintances, our family, and friends. The sense of belonging is one of our psychological needs as well. We feel comfortable in the native place, environment, and weather. The vampire of fear of solitude de-coffins when opportunities require us to leave our native environment, his bite produces indecisiveness.

Let me share a true story of an incredibly talented person,

"I Was a Nerd When I Was a Herd"

A Person got an excellent opportunity, which demanded to work in a different location. He had got the opportunity because of the quality he had delivered at his work, though he was excellent at his work, he got victimized by the 'herd mentality'.

Offered opportunity would have exposed him to new expertise and he would have been a person of greater value but struck by the vampire of fear of solitude he declined the opportunity.

Later, due to strategic reasons, his business unit was shut down, and business was off-shored. He ended up losing the job. He remained jobless for six months, learned his lesson after paying a hefty price, you should not do akin and prepare yourself pro-actively.

The good portion is that once he had learned his lesson, he used his reputation, called the Head Office and got appointed off-shores. Finally, he had to conquer his fear but under forced circumstances. Never in life wait for the circumstances to force you.

There is a phrase in Hindu Maha-Upanishad "Vasudhaiva Kutumbakam" which means "The World is

One Family." Today is the time of 'globalization' instead of feeling yourself a person belonging to one place, you must believe that the world is one family, and you are a member of this giant family. You must believe in "Vasudhaiva Kutumbakam." Once you truly accept this philosophy you will feel comfortable, you will grow irrespective of geographical and political borders.

Otherwise, you will not see the opportunities which exist beyond your sight. You will not be able to imagine what lies ahead and feel uncertain to march in that space.

5. **Vampire of Fear of What If:**

Many fears live in our mind, the "What If" fears-

What if, this happens – I might get hurt.

What if – I lose the comfort I have?

What if, that happens – I would never rise again.

What if, I do not succeed - people will criticize and laugh at me.

What if, it doesn't turn up right – I would be a loser.

An everlasting list, we love being more imaginative to find a logical excuse for our indecisiveness. After all, the feeling of not making a decision, without a logically dressed reason, is so uncomfortable, it causes nausea.

There are many reasons and fears to choose from and not take your chances. You must remember unless you take your first step, you do not begin your journey, forget about completing it.

The key here is to put the vampire of what-if fears aside and hit the stride. Take the opportunities which come your way, decide and move on. I will tell you about someone who did it:

In 1976, Indian Government was putting controls on a particular segment of Industry, the progress of people in that industry was to be impacted. At that time, a 26 years old valiant young man moved to Indonesia and opened his first factory there. There must have been many "what if" risks to stop him from taking this decision. The young man set the sail and went ahead, he walked on the path which made him the Chairman and CEO of world's largest steel producing company Arcelor Mittal.

In his own words - "Always think outside the box, and embrace opportunities that appear, wherever they might be."

Kick out the vampire of what-if fear from your life, you will feel safe, happy and more confident. Embrace the opportunities, continue until you start to create opportunities for others, this is how you can have a higher purpose in life.

6. <u>Vampire of Fear of Losing what we have</u>

If I do something new, I might lose what I already have. It is a common apprehension. We are so busy to handle our trivial belongings that we never think of the possibilities to create colossal things, for us and others. We are reluctant to accept new opportunities. We feel very comfortable with what we have. We need more but, we do not want the efforts which make us deserve more. We do not determine exactly what 'that more' or 'success' is for us.

Always define and quantify what success means to you.

We are comfortable to do the routine work, we are content with the returns we get. We do the same work year over year and do not want to learn new things. We want to hold the "so little" so close that fear of losing it holds us back to try new things. Most of the times, we remain inactive, live a stalled life, and do not make any progress.

We are so afraid to lose that, whenever we think about it; we torture ourselves with a very uncomfortable sentiment. We need to avoid this 'paralysis of analysis' for a successful life."

Patrick continues, "These are six vampires of fear which cause indecisiveness, we need to kill them all to be successful in life. Do you find this useful Vick?"

"Yes Pat, I find it useful, especially the vampire of fear of solitude and thinking big is crystal clear to me, I agree we need to move to new places and get opportunities wherever they appear. Success belongs to those, who prepare and present themselves to possibilities and have the eyes to see beyond the horizon. "Answers Victor.

"But I have questions related to vampires of fear of mistakes, failures, what if and losing- are those not real? And do these actually not impact us in life?"

Patrick: "Yes, you are on target Vick, let us take a new perspective then– fear of making mistakes, failures, what-if and losing, let us call it 'Fear to try new things and accept new opportunities.' Would you like to be a person, who is afraid to take new challenges? Success demands integrity within yourself, that internal strength of character which makes you stronger over time.

Why do you scare of people talking about you? There is a community of talkers who talk about everyone, they just need to talk as it is their appetite, when you fail they talk about it, when you succeed they still talk about it. The difference is, when you succeed, they follow you, respect you, and want to be like you. They approach you for an advice and guidance and request you to spare some time to motivate their kids or find a solution to a problem they face. It has happened to me, and you would also face similar situations soon."

The fear of mistakes, failures, and what-if, holds hardly any ground in reality.

Patrick pours his life's experiences and continues further,

"The fear to lose is a thought of an average mind, it makes you settle for an ordinary life, only to make both ends meet. Once you take chances and get success in your initial endeavors, the success ladder builds up higher and higher, by the end when you compare your proceeds, you laugh at yourself and say

"We have so much to gain and so little to lose, still we think about losing, this is loser's psychology."

You need to break the 'wall of Fears' with the hammer of 'Integrity within Yourself'. When you do it Vick, you take your first step towards success and abundance, then your efforts bless you with the right things in life.

As Sylvester Stallone expressed "I was an insecure kid. Once I saw 'Hercules' with Steve Reeves, it completely changed my life. If I had never gone to that film, I wouldn't be here today".

"Yes Pat, I understand now, we are afraid to lose so much that we forget that how much we can accomplish in life, I have same hours in my day and the same body, as of any other successful person, I do not have any disability. The difference is only the way successful people activate themselves– they integrate within, they develop a mechanism to handle fears, they do not get into confusions. Thus, they move more decisively and fearlessly.

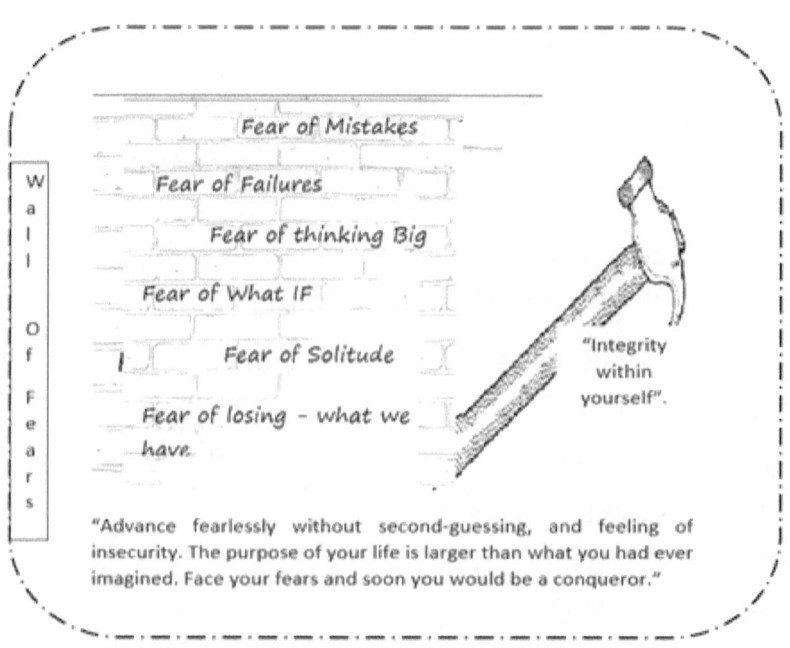

W
a
l
l

O
f

F
e
a
r
s

Fear of Mistakes

Fear of Failures

Fear of thinking Big

Fear of What IF

Fear of Solitude

Fear of losing - what we have.

"Integrity within yourself".

"Advance fearlessly without second-guessing, and feeling of insecurity. The purpose of your life is larger than what you had ever imagined. Face your fears and soon you would be a conqueror."

I need to take my chances, prove myself through results."

Victor thinks that he needs to learn as much as he can. He is keen to apply those concepts. He is very focused on the learnings imparted to him.

"That's incredible Pat, I thank you for the time taken out from a busy schedule and introducing me to this entirely new world of deep thinking."

"Deep thinking is the right word Vick, that's the misery. With the upsurge of information availability these days, people know everything, they can talk about any subject in length; but the usage of knowledge has become shallow, knowledge is spread more like rainwater, which dries up within a few hours or a day. Knowledge needs to be in-depth, like an ocean and we must know how to apply it", emphasizes Patrick.

Victor: "Yes, I do agree Pat."

Patrick: "Let's call it a day Vick. Yesterday, I spoke to a few of my acquaintances to help you find a job, and I do hope to get some response in a few weeks' time.

Now that you have learned the concept of Integrity within Yourself and 'Vampires of Fear', what do you think would follow next, any guess?

Victor: 'Integrity within Yourself' and 'Vampires of Fear' impact our decision making, isn't that logically leading towards something related to decision making, which is the key determiner of success?"

Patrick: "Not so fast Vick, "Decision Making –The Right Way" you would have to learn yourself. When you get a job, you will make decisions, and the right approach for decision making will ensure success in your initiatives. However, you will learn it by yourself, under practical scenarios."

Tomorrow, you will learn 'commitment to yourself' concept, continues Patrick

"After you go through the next conception, there would be a week's gap as I am traveling. By the time I am back, we might have a response to your job requests too. Please do not stop your own efforts, as more efforts produce more results."

Victor: "Thanks Pat, I am looking forward to the next concept of 'Commitment to yourself' and I will be eagerly waiting for your return. I will keep my efforts on."

Patrick: "May God bless you Vick, let us meet the day after tomorrow but at a different location this time, the place is sixty miles away from here, and you need to be there around five in the morning, here is the address. There is a particular reason to call you there." He continues, "There you will learn, the Commitment to Yourself concept." In the meantime think about why you should be a 'master of your skills' and Share your answers the in next meeting.

Victor: "Yes Pat, I will be there, and I will certainly come with a logical answer this time."

Victor thinks about the vampires of fear. He correlates those to various incidents he had seen in life.

Though he had not encountered all of the fears he could relate it to the people around. Next day, he visits a few more locations to submit his job applications.

Chapter – 4

"Commitment to yourself" concept.

The Vampire of non-commitment

"Unless commitment is made, there are only promises and hopes... but no plans." Peter Drucker

Victor wakes up at 3 AM. There is no sign of the Sun, it can be called midnight. There are few stars amidst the cloudy sky, and it is a full moon night, whenever the clouds uncover the moon, it appears as they play hide and seek, one shade of darkness follows another shade of silver moonlight.

"Wow it's a beautiful night" murmurs Vick, "I need to get ready and reach the location fast."

Patrick had told Victor how to reach there; and how much time it would take. Victor wants to reach there ahead of Patrick today. The location is on the highway, and it is not difficult to get a vehicle even at this hour. Victor can board a bus around 3.30 AM.

He whispers, "I will be there by 4.30 AM, earlier than Pat's arrival." He reaches the station and alights, much to his surprise Patrick has already reached there.

"Good morning Pat, I thought I would be reaching in advance of you today. But you are a winner, always" Victor cheerfully states.

Patrick smiles, "Yes, what makes me happy is to support you, reaching early is a sign of my commitment, and it brings me a sense of accomplishment.

Now, we need to march an hour to reach the destination. You would be meeting my guru today, who would bestow the concept of "Commitment to Yourself". It would be a refresher for me as well, he had guided me about seven years ago when I was struggling for success in career. When I applied the lessons he had given me, my life had instantly turned around."

Patrick reminds the question, "Now tell me, why you should be a Master in your Skills?"

Victor: Pat, I have given a deep thought to it, and I think that my answer would be able to convince you."

Patrick: "I am happy to hear that Vick, I am all ears."

Victor enthusiastically shares, "Mastery can be attained only by having in-depth knowledge of a subject, and knowledge has equipped man with the tremendous power, which makes one man lead others. Mastering skills bring power to life. No one can challenge the person, who has mastered his skills at the workplace. He attains leadership naturally and unquestioned."

"This is what I have come up with, after deliberating on this subject Pat."

Patrick meditated over his response for some time.

"Good answer Vick, can be better. Do you have more to add to what I would rate an average answer?"

"Not at this moment Pat, What do you think may be added to my reply to make it better? What approach should we follow here? Do you agree with my answer or do you have an entirely different opinion on it"? Perplexes, Victor.

Patrick raises his hand and replies: "Yes, I have a different view on this, you know the value but not the purpose. I assent that mastery is power, which generates authority, but we must use it for the improvement of humanity. We live in the times where authorities come with a superior responsibility. We master skills not only to be powerful but also to help needy people. With the skills we have, we can contribute to make things and lives better, find solutions and create new ways and means for everyone."

He continues and the voice comes from deep within, his feelings flow through his words. "When you start to work, your education of 15 or 18 years is not useful, because you have yet to learn its practical applications.

So far, you have only read literature and never applied it.

Tell me, If you help others in examinations, by telling the answers, solving their problems, it would be called cheating, isn't it?"

"Yes, that's correct, it's cheating," echoed Victor while they inch toward the destination.

Patrick: "This is the rule for academics, it changes when you enter into corporate life. What has considered cheating in schools becomes a critical success factor in the organization – you need to help people, you need to work as a fantastic team player, personal excellence is appreciated only when it contributes toward team projects and joint initiatives. Mastery of your skills helps you to find faster and better solutions for your colleagues, company, and its customers.

The vampire follows you when you still play the corporate sport with college game rules. In a nutshell, your skills belong to serve a bigger purpose, encompassing others. Knowledge is only a potential power unless you put it in action, the right way."

"Hope you understand this, Vick."

Victor reciprocates, "The rules change when we switch from one sport to another. Winning depends on working as a strong team and contributing at our best skillset levels, helping where we are strong, passing it to others on their call, where they have the strength.

Using the power of skills with the responsibility to help those around us, this is what you mean Pat, right?"

Patrick: "Yes, correct Vick, you got it right."

They reach half way across the well-trodden path which serves as a short-cut to the place where they have to meet the guru.

"Vick, what do you think about soldiers?"

Victor: "This time I have to get it right Pat, soldiers are the pride of a nation. They protect the honor of our country with their commitment, sacrifice so that we can live peacefully with our families. They stay away from their homes and take positions in the war zones, glaciers, borders, oceans and everywhere to secure our motherland. Their duties bring out the best in them— courage, discipline, team spirit and loyalty. These days, ideal soldiers must be not only physically fit but also have balanced interests. They are not machines that obey orders, they are brave and intelligent men who will follow only with understanding - they know why they have to obey. They understand the bigger purpose of their lives. A lot of my neighbors were in armed forces, and I understand how they are our Heroes."

"I hope this answer is close to your expectation Pat? I think very highly of them."

Patrick smiles, "That's coming along nicely, I echo what you just mentioned, and I am satisfied with your reply with no value-add from my side, this time."

Patrick chuckles, "But do you know, why I asked this question all of a sudden?"

"I have no idea Pat, why you asked this, but I am happy to know that you are satisfied with my response, I feel slowly I am getting there. I am getting acquainted with the larger purpose of life. Would you please tell me what prompted that question?"

The time at this moment is 5.15 AM and Patrick tells Victor that they are about half an hour ahead of schedule and need to wait on the way. His appointment with his guru has fixed at 6 AM in the morning. Both sit on a bench placed for passengers to rest. The bright rays of the sun spread across the fields. The birds chirp as though teaching a crucial lesson of life- why they wake up early and from where the phrases "early-bird" and "Early bird catches the worm" derive from.

Patrick answers, "What prompted the question, is the fact that my guru is a retired senior ranking army official and as you summarized about their commitment, sacrifice, courage, discipline, team spirit and loyalty, who can be a better person to coach you about the concept of "commitment to yourself" than him? It would help you to kill the vampire of non-commitment. He headed troops during major wars, assured strategic victories over enemies, and won many gallantry awards. The President honored his audacity and leadership on the battle ground. He is **Colonel Michael Barr**, who now lives a retired life on the outskirts, away from the hustle and bustle of the city. He still continues to serve the nation through his guidance to the youth who seek."

Patrick and Victor start to walk again. They reach Colonel Barr's home at 5.55 AM. The premises of Colonel's home spreads approximately ten thousand square yards with a well maintained organic garden, patios-furniture, a three seater swing, everything made of golden-brown teakwood. It adds a graceful look to the surroundings. Exactly at 5.59 AM Patrick rings the doorbell, ding dong.

In a few moments, they hear the sound of footsteps inside the home, marching toward the door. Colonel Michael Barr opens the door.

Victor meets Colonel Barr for the first time. Colonel is well built, six foot five inches tall, with broad chest and shoulders. His curved mustaches adore the glory of his chivalry which Patrick had shared a few moments back. Straight back, gray and full hair, graciously styled. He smiles and looks at them with sparky eyes.

Patrick advances "Good Morning Sir, we are here, thanks for giving us time from your busy schedule."

Colonel greets them, "Welcome, young men, I was waiting for both of you, and Pat, he must be Victor about whom you had spoken to me."

His voice is resonant and deep which generates a fascinating effect on Victor. He imagines about a splendid meeting.

"Yes Sir, he is Victor, he is here in search of the work and I am imparting him the lessons which you gave me during my early career. As I promised to help needy people around me with my knowledge, I am here with him. He is privileged to have a chance to be groomed by you, and learn the terrific concept of "Commitment to yourself" from its originator himself. It would also act as a refresher for me, and we are incredibly excited to be here." Patrick expresses with a beaming smile on his face.

Colonel offers them seats nearby the center table of the grand living room. Victor glances around, high roof, decorated walls adorned the glories of a War Hero, and all witnessed the larger than life person who served the nation. Photographs that belonged to victories of wars, multiple medallions, shields and the various certificates of bravery from Army Chiefs and Presidents. The room is filled with so much courage and zeal.

Colonel sits with his back straight and applauds, "That's spectacular my boy, I feel so proud to see you grow, and achieve your goals. It also gives me immense pleasure that now you have a larger purpose and higher commitment level in life. It is commendable that you have also ensured to help others while staying focused on your goals.

The commitment of life is to make our life better, and while doing so, add value to the life of those around us. It is not about how much we can take from but also how much we can contribute to the world. Only then we can make this world a better place to live, grow and flourish.

Victor, welcome to the new world. I understand that Patrick has already taught you the concepts of Integrity within yourself and Fears of Decisions making. I will take you through the concept of commitment to yourself and would expect you to help others as you move forward in life."

"Thank you, Sir, I feel incredibly honored to be with an eminent person like you. I need to admit that I never had an opportunity to be around a person who has contributed so much to the country. I am very passionate to learn about the concept of Commitment to Yourself" Victor chimes in a flow, almost breathless.

"Life isn't about finding yourself. Life is about creating yourself." G. B. Shaw.

Colonel quotes G.B Shaw, "Life is about creating yourself, we need to create a strong – character and philosophy. Our current actions will carve the path for future success, we cannot create it without the principle of 'Commitment to Yourself'. I have followed this principle throughout my life and will preserve till my journey is complete.

Most people need continuous push throughout life. They always want motivation from friends, parents, circumstances, bosses and relatives. They actually do not live but drag their lives. It's like you have a Ferrari and instead to start the engine, you drag it to the other end of the city.

How will you complete your journey? What is the purpose of having a Ferrari? What is the benefit of foolish hard-work? In their view they have really worked hard and are unlucky to get results.

To have a splendid journey, you need to ignite the engine and then drive it, toward the destination. You will reach faster.

To have a superb life, we must ignite our brain and commit that I will drive my life, rather than drag it. Push makes you reach up to a certain distance, self-drive gets you to the destination.

That's why the results go bad for the children, who do not get a consistent push, by the parents or teachers. It is okay till they are too naive, however when they can think, read and their brain can process information, they must not need a push, and spark their brain to drive the life.

There are people who, to wake up at 8 AM in the morning, set the alarm at 6 AM, then keep putting it off till 8 AM. Even after this, they still need ten minutes more to catch up on sleep. Finally, they wake up late, and then there is so much hurry to get ready, run for office or school. They make mistakes on the way, reach late at the destination. Being late gives a bad first impression. This ten minutes delay can end up missing the buses, flights and opportunities too.

Why all this? They do not commit to themselves, that is why they cannot make it. Such people can never be successful. Waking up at a certain time is a commitment you do to yourself, not to anybody else.

It impacts your personality and character, not only you make a fake self-commitment but you also get comfortable to break it every day. In each instance your subconscious brain receives a message – I have committed, but I know, it will not matter if I do not do it. You end up create a shallow personality.

If we cannot honor a little commitment made to self, we must know what will be the results of the commitments to others. There are many promises and commitments we make and break ourselves – to drop few extra pounds, study hard, quit smoking and alcohol, read and exercise 30 minutes a day, complete pending tasks, and the list goes on.

We do not care about breaking commitments because it becomes a constituent of our personality. Our subconscious brain trains over the years to accept this behavior.

The solution is simple, if you have to wake up at 8 AM, put the alarm for 8 AM and wake up at the first bell. It's very simple to follow, but cannot be done if 'Commitment to Yourself' is absent. Do not commit if you cannot honor."

Colonel pauses for a moment, while Victor recalls; how much problems he had in the past, because of this issue. He could have easily fixed it but he had made no efforts, his outcomes were average because he needed a constant push. Unknowingly I was damaging my character every day.

Colonel continues further, "It is easy to do this son, and it has an everlasting impact, the people who follow this consistently craft path of success. Non-commitment might not matter to the people not connected with you, but when you are in a relation whether official or personal, it impacts a lot. It matters to the nation which provides for your needs and to your family.

Everyone likes committed people, they see trust, hope, deliverance, confidence and future in them, and feel confident around them. They are the one, to be called out first when an opportunity knocks at the door.

Richard Branson is an excellent example of 'commitment to yourself' he faced hardships, when he was a kid he had dyslexia and his educational performance was bad as a student. Despite all this from an early age he wanted to be a businessman, at the age of sixteen he started his first endeavor – A magazine called 'Student'. Over the time he was able to develop the character-strength, which was robust enough to help him rise and become the pride of the country. His commitment spread beyond him and benefitted entire masses, today, he is one of the most stirring business barons. He has founded the Virgin Group, which controls more than four hundred syndicates and he serves many humanitarian causes. He killed the vampire of troublesome youth and emerged as an ultimate conqueror.

There are countless instances.

If you practice 'commitment to yourself', the path of success will automatically follow. You will be able to kill the vampire of non-commitment and create glorious value for everyone. Success or failure is a byproduct of the acts you do, day in, day out.

Once you commit my son, you will emerge as an eternal winner.

'Commitment to yourself.'
Always

     I will live the life of high ethics and values.
     I will continuously work to upgrade my skills.
     I will apply what I have learned, for the refinement of mankind.
     I will accept, rectify and not repeat mistakes.
     I will value time, money, people and nation.
     I will win over my fears and stay determined.
     I will never lose hope.
     I will keep myself physically and mentally fit.
     I will honor my words and not make excuses.
     I will create solutions for myself and help others.
     I will be a team player and be part of bigger objectives.
     I will make a difference and consistent efforts.

I will communicate fearlessly but listen empathetically.

And my son, one commitment to me, that you will always remember "commitment to yourself." Now, if you have any questions, please feel free to ask. "

Colonel offers them coffee and discusses his war memories, how soldiers use to give moral, physical and mental courage to peer soldiers. The Brotherhood and unwavering commitment they demonstrate, when the bullets pass over their heads, sometimes hitting them. They always show grander determination, even when the bombs explode on their sides. A strong commitment toward the dream of their country. It is because of their dedication that our nation remains dominant and grows. In the absence of commitment, the situation would have been different. Self-commitment alters the future of your life and all aspects related to it.

Colonel clarifies their questions, Vick takes notes to follow the principle. He feels delighted and then both leave for home.

Commitment is what transforms a promise into a reality... Commitment is the stuff character is made of;

the power to change the face of things. It is the daily triumph of integrity over skepticism. – Abraham Lincoln.

Chapter – 5

"Eight Internal Happiness Scenarios."

The Vampire of unhappiness

"We begin from the recognition that all beings cherish happiness and do not want suffering. It then becomes both morally wrong and pragmatically unwise to pursue only one's own happiness oblivious to the feelings and aspirations of all others who surround us as members of the same human family. The wiser course is to think of others when pursuing our own happiness."

- *Dalai Lama*

On the way back, Patrick states, "We still have four hours to reach home, on the way I will tell you a secret, which uniquely helped me a lot, and it is this secret, which has benefitted faster."

"I will share the 'Eight Internal happiness scenarios' – how to multiply them and succeed in life."

Victor wonders, what the eight inner happiness secrets are and how they can multiply. His family always told him to be happy, but he does not know how happiness increases.

He looks at Patrick with luminous eyes, "I am very keen to know, who on the planet doesn't want to be happy. That is the ultimate goal, whatever we do, the end-product we need is happiness."

Patrick shares, "Success doesn't always produce happiness, but happiness produces success."

"Let me list the eight internal happiness scenarios, where an average person feels happy in a lifetime, there are no more than eight scenarios. I am talking about 'inner happiness' as it is produced within you and is not dependent on external factors.

If you find additional situations on your journey of life, please share those with me as well.

You feel internally happy when you:
    H1 Pass Major Examinations/accomplishments
    H2 Fall in love
    H3 Get first pays cheque
    H4 Get a Promotion as a recognition of your contributions
    H5 Buy your Assets (Home/Car)
    H6 Hold you newly born baby

H7 Do something excellent for others

H8 Cherish your hobbies

So if you want to be happy, there are only a limited occasions.

To be successful, you need to be happy. Happiness creates an aura, in which opportunities surround you. Happiness makes you attractive irrespective of your appearance, and people would love to be in your company.

Further, he pulls a paper from his pocket and shares an article published by The American Psychological Association (APA),

"Happy individuals are predisposed to seek out and undertake new goals in life and this reinforces positive emotions, say researchers who examined the connections between desirable characteristics, life successes and well-being of over two hundred and seventy thousand people.

Lead author Sonja Lyubomirsky, Ph.D., of the University of California, Riverside found that chronically happy people are in general more successful across many life domains than less happy people and their happiness is in large part a consequence of their positive emotions rather than vice versa. Happy people are more likely to achieve favorable life circumstances, said Dr. Lyubomirsky, and "this may be because happy people frequently experience positive moods and these positive moods prompt them to be more likely to work actively toward new goals and build new resources. When people feel happy, they tend to feel confident, optimistic, and energetic and others find them likable and sociable. Happy people are thus able to benefit from these perceptions.

Much of the previous research on happiness presupposed that happiness followed from success and accomplishments in life.

Our review provides strong support that happiness, in many cases, leads to successful outcomes, rather than merely following from them, "and happy individuals are more likely than their less happy peers to have fulfilling marriages and relationships, high incomes, superior work performance, community involvement, robust health and even a longer life."

"Hope you are getting the point, Vick – happiness turns the switch of success on, with the help of actions you take." Patrick stops and looks at Victor.

Victor "Yes Pat, I have always felt happy in the company of happy people, I used to laugh, do funny things and when I recall those memories even today, I feel happy again. I would like to be happy throughout my life and impart the same feeling to people around me. You can count on me for that."

"But, if we only have eight scenarios to be happy in this extensive journey of life, how can these be sufficient to stay happy forever?"

He looks at Patrick, eagerly waiting for the response.

"You got the point Vick, this is where the 'multiplication of happiness' applies. In your life you come across many people, some people hold a permanent space in your life.

The rule is simple –If you have five-person in your life, have a devoted and genuine relation with them, the level of relationship should be such that their eight happiness scenarios become your own happiness scenarios. This multiplication will yield forty additional happiness instances in your life. This simple rule will increase your happy moments.

We will go into a minute detail for happiness scenarios, and you would be able to figure out how to do the 'multiplication' in your life.

Pass Major Examinations/Accomplishment – this stops once you stop to learn and unless you begin again, it remains so. Most of the people do not turn back to books after they leave formal education and especially to structured courses, so this reason dies. They close the door of happiness– if you want to multiply this happiness, continue learning.

When you fall in love – This stops when you start to take your beloved for granted and lose the feeling of love over time. Continue to love and express your feelings to your loved ones to multiply it. You will notice the magnitude of happiness which increases.

"Being deeply loved by someone gives you strength while loving someone deeply gives you courage" - Lao Tzu

Get your first pay cheque– This love is short lived as it becomes routine and if you do not do well, you start to complain about your payment. To multiply it you must love your work, instead to love job security. Add more value to your job and the pay cheque will automatically increase from time to time and multiply your happiness. Look for opportunities across the globe in case it does not work out at your current location. If you develop and excel in your job, your pay cheque would also replicate the same, it too will increase.

Get a Promotion as a recognition of your contributions – we feel fantastic when we earn respect and recognition through our contributions. To multiply it, increase your contributions – promotions and rewards are a byproduct.

When you buy Assets (Home) – To multiply this upgrade yourself with your growth. Lots of people feel happy when they buy a car, jewelry. Do it for your own happiness not due to peer pressure.

To hold your new-born baby - To multiply this, love your kids even when they are grown up. Do this throughout life, and that too without any expectation of returns. Your happiness will multiply when you watch them succeed and live a happy life.

Do something excellent for others – This will increase your happiness, you will have a greater sense of accomplishment. There is no greater satisfaction than to see everyone jovial and flourish around you, help them in the moment of crisis. As Mother Teresa suggested, "Spread love everywhere you go. Let no one ever come to you without leaving happier". Mother Teresa received several honors, including the 1979 Nobel Peace Prize.

Cherish your hobbies – This is one of the most important measures. Whenever you spend the time to pursue your hobbies, may it be travel, read, sing, dance, swim, hike, help, paint, write or whatever you love to do, your happiness multiplies. Practice and repeat these hobbies daily. Remember 'commitment to yourself', do not make excuses of not to get time, most people drop their hobbies once they enter into professional life.

In the meantime put a full stop to evil happiness like excessive shopping, alcoholism, smoking and using credit money."

As Jim Rohn told, "Happiness is not something you postpone for the future; it is something you design for the present."

"I can guarantee that, when you are genuinely happy in the happiness of others, you remain happy at all the times. You are different from rest of the people in the world, which feel sad and jealous when others are happy and succeed, they trap themselves in a negative mental frame and finally collapse because of the venom of jealousy inside them.

When you look around, you will find that people are unhappy because of the success of others, students are unhappy when other student scores better, they are unhappy because someone does better than them. People are unhappy when a colleague is appreciated and rewarded more for the contributions.

This behavior is very ugly, to break this habit think inverse, and put yourself in the shoes of a successful person – would you like people to hate your success, your achievements? If you want them to be happy in your success, you should also learn to be happy in their success."

Victor raises a question, "Pat, don't you think it is easier said than done? Is it not difficult to stay happy in the happiness of others when it is not yours?"

Patrick "When you begin it looks difficult later it makes you a virtuoso. Remember a few points of 'commitment to yourself.

> I will win over my fears and remain determined.
> I will value time, money, people and nation.
> I will create solutions for myself and help humankind.
> I will be a team player and part of bigger objectives.
> I will make a difference.

If you live up to your commitments and value people, create solutions, become a team player and consider yourself as part of bigger objectives, and if you desire to make a difference, you will have to embrace other's happiness. This fear is notional, this timid and self-centered attitude will not work. You would be directionless and spend more time to think about the other's success instead of carving your own path of happiness which attracts success.

'You must not dream, a bigger or better life with a petite heart and a bad attitude.'

I hope you understand the significance of this, I have applied this, and people around me get impressed with my genuine happiness in their success. Support them during the crisis. You need to be sincere and trustworthy for the people in your company. When you work with them, you get the best support and they like to be with you for a longer span.

Let me tell you story of Professor Satish Dhawan, the then Chairman of Indian Space Research Organization. Under him, Dr. APJ Kalam was a project director. The mission was to put India's satellite into orbit. Many teams and thousands of members worked together to achieve the goal.

On the day of launch, a few parts went out of order, still they ignored the computer warnings and launched it manually. The satellite instead of going into orbit fell into the Bay of Bengal, the launch turned out to be a huge disaster.

That day,   Prof. Satish Dhawan, called a press conference, journalists from across the world joined it. Prof. Dhawan took the lead and conducted the press conference himself. He shouldered entire responsibility for the failure, he understood that his team had worked very hard, but needed more technological support. He assured the media that soon the team would make another attempt and will definitely succeed. Professor Dhawan took accountability and saved Dr. Kalam from the embarrassment of failure.

Next year, in July 1980, it was the time to relaunch the satellite, this time, it was successful. In preparation for the press conference, Prof. Dhawan called Dr. Kalam and instructed, 'You conduct the press conference today.'

When the mission failed he took entire responsibility and when it succeeded, he gave complete credit to the team. Professor Dhawan is the right example of having a genuine relationship with people, an exemplary relationship that can be trusted. He was happy in the success of his team, wanted them to take credit and was there to protect them during the crisis.

Success followed after success, Dr. APJ Abdul Kalam later became the President of India, also known as the 'Missile Man' and 'People's President.'

You need to have genuine relationships to have such an impact on the life of people, and that will keep you happy forever."

Victor appreciates the answer and concept of happiness, his eyes fill with emotions after listening to the story. He gets convinced that he must not dream, a bigger or better life with a tiny heart and a bad attitude. He commits to himself, I will always practice this. They continue to walk.......

Patrick has plans to fly next morning. Before leaving, he says, "Vick, although I am recommending you for a job, the company may or may not select you, unless you show delightful aptitude and attitude in the interview. They have various criteria like Integrity, self-discipline, necessary qualifications, skill set, attitude, willingness, inner strength, and cost, etc. I am setting the expectations right so that you do not feel disappointed later.

Please answer their questions confidently and apply the wisdom you have learned these days."

"I will do my best, "replies Victor.

He reaches home, he could not sleep that night, and kept thinking about the learnings he recently had 'Commitment to Yourself' and 'Eight internal happiness scenarios' – How to multiply and succeed. He also goes through the notes to learn from "Integrity within yourself" and "Fears of Decision-making."He commits always to remember and apply these learnings in life.

Next week he revisits the placement agencies, searches local newspapers, and speaks to a few companies which have posted the job requirements on the notice boards. He does not tire to make applications multiple times.

He lives up to the concepts and he makes consistent efforts. Within that week, he drops as many applications as he could.

To visit various places and interact with new people adds to his knowledge. When he had arrived here, he used to think this was a gigantic city for any individual to get lost, now he gets familiar with it.

Victor is in the city for three months yet he has not been able to find a job. He is about to run out of cash too, but he is motivated enough to take on the vampires now. He is sure that he will succeed. Simultaneously, he waits for Patrick's return from the trip and to hear about the response from the people Patrick had spoken to."

So far, he gets no calls from the companies where he had applied.

"It's the repetition of affirmations that leads to belief. And once that belief becomes a deep conviction, things begin to happen." -Muhammad Ali

He reads the notes of the learnings from Patrick and Colonel Michael Barr. His conscious and subconscious brain slowly start to come in unison.

"If your conscious and subconscious mind are in synchronization, your deeds match words."

Chapter – 6

"Painful but Gainful Experience"
The Vampire of Weak Internal Communication

Before success comes in any man's life, he's sure to meet with much temporary defeat and, perhaps some failures. When defeat overtakes a man, the easiest and the most logical thing to do is to quit. That's exactly what the majority of men do. - *Napoleon Hill*

Patrick comes back after a week. They had already decided the place to meet before he left for the trip. Victor is hopeful for a positive response from the people where Patrick had referred him.

He was in Japan last week, so Victor inquires, "How was your trip, Pat?"

Patrick explains, "It was incredibly wonderful Vick. Japan is astonishingly affluent. The first impression you have after arrival is that it is impeccable and clean, not even a cigarette butt on roadsides. There is no sign of scarcity, dust, or illness. Japanese believe in Kaizen which means - continuous improvement of working practices, personal efficiency, removing the defects with a consistent and continuous problem-solving approach. It's a wonderful place to visit, work and live.

How was your week and what you did?"

"Well, I continued my journey of job hunting, have submitted my improved resume and applications at many places" Victor shows his notebook. He had listed all contact details and addresses where he made the job applications.

"Your handwriting is terrific Vick. The information you have written in your notebook is valuable.

I have wonderful news to share with you, the places where I had recommended you, two of those companies have called you for an interview next week.

Their offices are around thirty-five miles from here. You have to go there on Monday and Wednesday. Both companies are located adjacent to each other.

I hope your wait for job search may be over now, I will keep my fingers crossed. Here are a few basic tips that I will give you to be more efficient in the interviews.

Pay particular attention to your presentation, the clothes should not be mandatorily new, but must be neat, ironed and remember to wear formals. Some companies allow semi-formals these days but the companies where you will appear for the interview are in the service sector, and they pay particular attention to your appearance. Shoes must be polished. Be comfortable and confident while you answer the questions. Remember, this is your first meeting with your prospective employer, and it's pivotal to have a pleasant first impression.

The interview is an assessment process and they will evaluate you on all parameters of the job requirement. Focus on your strengths, and make use of what you have learned so far."

Patrick hands over a note which includes the details of time, address, phone numbers, and the name of persons he has to meet for the interview.

"I wish you luck Vick, and do your best. I will pray for your success.

It will be an excellent idea to go and observe the place on Sunday so that you have no difficulty to reach in time on interview day."

Victor felt indebted to his angel, and he had carefully listened to the tips given. Usually, people do not get such support in a new place. They feel alone as they do not have anyone to share the pain. His new learnings, generate a deep sense of relaxation for the first time after he had reached in the city.

"I am very grateful to you Pat, I will keep my nerves under control, visit the place on Sunday and do my best. Thanks for your precious guidance and advice".

"I do need a thanks Vick. When you become successful in life, always help people who are in need. There are so many individuals who do not know what to do under such situations."

"It would be great to be able to pass on to someone all of the successes, the failures, and the knowledge that one has had. To help someone, avoid all the fire, pain and anxiety would be wonderful. -Sylvester Stallone"

"I promise as per the commitment to yourself - I will create solutions for myself and help others." Replies Victor.

"Once again, all the best Vick, may God bless you."

On Sunday, Victor wakes up at dawn, he prays, gets ready and heads to the location of his first prospective employer. As Patrick had mentioned the place is thirty-five miles away, but it is outside the city, connects with a link road, with rare transport connectivity. On Sunday there is hardly any movement, another person also stands at the bus stop where the link road began.

Victor checks with him, "Sir, would you help me to know, how to get to this place, do any buses go there at regular intervals?" He shows him the address.

The stranger replies "No, there is no bus connectivity to that place on weekends, there are minibusses every fifteen minutes which go there in the morning hours, from 8 to 10 AM and evening 6 to 9 PM that too, only Monday to Friday. Most people use their own vehicles to reach there."

Victor understands why Patrick had advised him to visit the place a day in advance, he asks further
"So how do we get there on weekends?"

The other person replies, "Man, if you are lucky you get a lift from any gentleman who goes in that direction or any goods carrier which will charge, a trivial amount to drop you there."

He and the stranger signal for the lift, one lorry stops, and finally, he reaches the place where both the companies are located.

Though the distance was only thirty-five miles it had taken him around two and a half hour to reach there. He notes, "Travel time does not relate to the distance in all cases, it depends on how the place connects." It had taken lesser time to reach Colonel's place which is around 60 miles.

In the afternoon he comes back, it is a scorching hot day. It felt as the Sun conveyed a message- efforts produce sweat, sweat produces results. On the way back the sole of his right shoe cracks. What a pity!
He gets a wagon in return, which drops him at the beginning of link road where he had started his journey that morning. He first goes to repair his shoe, his money is about to finish.
By evening, he is back to his place. He has not written to his mother in these three months. There are phone booths, but calls are expensive so to write a letter is the only alternative.

He writes a letter to his mother,

"Dear Mom,

Hope you are in sound health. It's been three months since I am here and I have not written to you. I want to tell you that I miss you a lot, I miss all the pats and cuddles you have given me. I miss the moments when you assured, everything is going to be alright. I miss the moments when you encouraged me, believed in me, and let me know that you never expected more than the best I could do. Thank you for teaching me to see the positive aspect under all circumstances. Thanks for feeding me, and for the nights you didn't sleep because I was sick. There were times when I couldn't walk as a child because my little feet were tired, you carried me despite your own weakness. Thank you for that too.

Thank you for the unconditional love and care you showered on me, at all times. I can never thank you enough for the pain you tolerated to bring me into this world.

Mom, I know you are eagerly waiting to know what I have done in these three months. First of all, rest assured, I am in the company of good people and am learning new things. I have applied at many places for a job, but there are no upshots so far. This week I have been called for two interviews, and I am hopeful that something amazing will happen soon.

I feel apologetic to say mom, that the money, which I had carried with me, would be finished by next week. Please send me some more money, as that would be necessary to continue my mission here.

I commit to you, one day I will succeed and would become a pillar of strength for my family and all. I am determined.

I LOVE YOU MOM – Your Vick".

The Interviews

The first interview is on the next day, Victor irons his white shirt, gray trousers, goes through the notes one last time, and refreshes lessons. He makes a point to read the notes daily as Zig Ziglar coached "People often say that motivation doesn't last. Well, neither does bathing - that's why we recommend it daily." It keeps him mentally strong and motivated.

While he wears his shoes, he looks at the sole which he had got mended yesterday, he notices that it does not laugh at him but says "Everything will be OK soon, I am there to support you, stride with confident steps Vick." With his earlier attitude, he would have found it mocking at him and saying "Let's see, how many more days will you last."

He reminisces the days whenever his father brought a new pair of shoes and he slept wearing those.

The power of positive mind is the capability to find good under all circumstances.

He confidently heads to the venue. The interview has scheduled at eleven in the morning.

Victor reaches half an hour earlier than the interview time, there he watches six more candidates who had applied for the same position. He is there with Patrick's reference, the chances for him are high. Sharp at eleven the HR Manager calls him. Though Victor has all the learnings with him, he feels afraid and nervous when he enters the room. All this time he has reminded himself about the concepts and this offered him strength.

The interviewer is a knowledgeable and kind person, he makes Victor comfortable.

He replies to all questions tactfully and the interviewer satisfies with the answers. He puts remarks on Victor's resume, keeps it with him and asks to wait till all other interviews get over. He informs Victor that there will be a second round for shortlisted candidates with Department Head; and the Branch Head will make the final selection. So he has two more rounds to qualify for the position.

The interviews finish around 3.30 PM, in the meantime discussions between other candidates continue, a couple of them belonged to well-to-do families. Victor finds that most of the candidates are as directionless as he was earlier to interactions with Patrick and Colonel. The learnings have made a difference.

A good news comes, Victor is on the list with two other candidates for the second round and he is the first one to appear there as well.

The department head is a middle-aged person, lines on his face represent of responsibilities he handles.

Victor feels more optimistic, his anxiety has disappeared by this time. He replies to all questions wisely and Department Head impresses with the way Victor handles the questions. Everything goes well.

Suddenly, a new question,

"Victor, you have adequately replied to the questions, I feel you are an excellent candidate. However, our office has located in outskirts of the city. Your job would need you to visit field areas as well. We prefer employees who own vehicles. I presume that you have your own vehicle to commute."

Victor neither had a vehicle nor the money to buy it. He knew his family's financial condition very well, and he was aware that they would not be able to afford one. Victor could not make till the final round of interview.

Unfortunately, the second interview on Wednesday meets a similar fate, this time, the reason remains different.

Selected candidate was referred by a Director in the company so he couldn't succeed here as well. He comes back after he finishes the interviews, also he keeps himself positive and handles the pressure. It becomes a painful but gainful experience

> *"Life is 10 percent what happens to you and ninety percent how you respond to it." – Lou Holtz*

He reminds himself the 'commitment to yourself' -"I will make a difference and make consistent efforts.

"I will never lose hope, I will never lose hope, I will never lose hope."He reinforces.

By this time he knows that he needs to make more efforts to achieve his goal. He feels satisfied that he had passed on individual criteria. Though the situation is unfavorable, he communicates himself to prepare for future. By this time, his mother had sent him money with a tiny note –Son, I love you too, and I have full faith in you – you will succeed for sure.

The benefit of positive internal communication is priceless, it's like a diamond which you get for free.

It directly touches your opinion and creates the life you want. It helps you to concentrate on a solution instead to focus on negatives. Our brain acts as a magnet, it attracts what we think. To attract good we need to think about it but do note that in the absence of plans and action, there is no superlative use of it. Remember that thinking is the first step, planning is the second and action is the third. Do TPA – Think Plan Action to get a PAT – Prize Appreciation Triumph!

Your positive internal communications continuously motivate you to make best efforts. You win over your current problems, and prepare to face the vampires to success as well. Nothing in this world can bring you down. When the situation is against you, nothing works in your favor, the best support you can give is to stand with yourself and engage in positive internal communication. Problems are gravely afraid of strong people. They only take down the weaker and confused. Have you ever heard a goat killed the lion? If you practice positive internal communication, you become bigger than your problems. They will be afraid to face you and finally move out of your way. *Frank Outlaw has wisely said, "Watch your thoughts, they become words; watch your words, they become actions; watch your actions, they become habits; watch your habits, they become character; watch your character, for it becomes your destiny."*

Chapter – 7

"On your marks; Get, Set and Go."

The Vampire of Doing Average efforts

"A little more persistence, a little more effort, and what seemed hopeless failure may turn to glorious success."-
Elbert Hubbard

Victor updates Patrick on the fate of his first two interviews. Patrick reassures, "We will make more efforts, I will let you know about more opportunities as soon as I get any information, in the meantime, continue to revisit what you have learned so far and do not lose focus. As Paul J Meyer wisely said, 'Do a little bit more than average and from that point on our progress multiplies itself out of all proportion to the effort put in."

"Yes, I promise, I will make consistent efforts and will never lose hope." reaffirms Victor

He remembers a fable, **"Mango Millionaire"** his mother told once,

The wealthiest man in the town was old and wise, he guided the youths the ways to gain riches, and he was called Mango-Millionaire. Once a boy asked him, "What is the reason you became so rich? Were your forefathers rich? Did they pass any wealth to you?" He chuckled, "My forefathers lived by meager means, and they had got no spare pennies". He pointed toward a tree, "When my father died, he asked me to take care of the mango tree, he whispered that this is the only wealth I have, and I pass it to you, after he breathed last. I was too young, to understand his message but I tried, initially I sold mangos which were few, then I discovered the new way to make recipes and shakes. As the wise said, a penny saved is a penny earned, initially I saved each of them, and then I saw they did not grow in hideouts. I took the money and used it to expand my work, had some losses but learned with time. Those stumbling blocks could not hold me back, people started to believe in my ideas and products and after that there was no looking back."

Moral: Keep working until you achieve, think of new ideas. When an idea gets combined with action, miracles happen.

At this time, Victor determines to make several efforts to accomplish the goal for which he had come to the city. He continues that, with more inner strength, and on a daily basis.

His life is about to change, the place is about to change, he is about to begin a new journey, in the direction his mentors have coached him. He is about to develop his own concepts. At this time, he has no cognizance that he is about to embark on a journey which will transform hundreds of lives through his vision, help, and guidance.

The real breakthrough

Next day, he receives a call letter from one of the companies he had applied three weeks ago, they want to interview him, in the following week.

Victor prepares for the interview, he is on the path of continuous improvement. The day of interview arrives, the objective of this company is to bring the costs down. They look for fresh candidates, who can work at a low cost. Bringing costs down has become a detestable vampire globally, and it results in offshoring, outsourcing, and downsizing. The company is ready to go through the painful process to train fresh graduates.

He repeats the earlier sequence, he visits the place a day before and reports for the interview in time. By evening, he comes to know about the decision.

The interviewers select him with more positive remarks in comparison to other recruits. The salary offered is hardly sufficient to make both ends meet, but he plans to survive with adjustments like to share the accommodation, shift to a closer location and save commuting cost. He can manage as there were three other new hires who are willing to stay together. They tell Victor that he will be given due training to handle the job.

This job becomes his Launchpad to the corporate world, to take-off and never look back.

First few days, appearance vs. reality:

"There's a certain type of fear that if somebody believes differently from me, it's a threat. Because I'm right, and there cannot be two ways that are right, so if I'm right, anything different than this must be wrong; and we attack those things and it's really due to insecurity, ego and fear." - Radhanath Swami

Now, Victor's most cherished dream has come true and he enters in the real corporate world. He joins as an office assistant. His primary responsibility is to assist another person to manage work.

He changes the place he lives and moves to a location closer to his workplace. Back home, he goes to meet and share the good news with Patrick, but he finds him out of the city. He cannot personally inform his angel that the goal for which they have worked so intensely, is accomplished, he leaves a message at his home.

The corporate life is an entirely different world. Instead of formal training, he and his three friends get assignments with four different teams. His senior, mostly rests lost in the files, computer systems and phone calls from clients, always in a hurry and worry. He handles several responsibilities and work pressures.

Victor notices that his senior focuses to complete the tasks, always on top of his work. Consequently, he has no time to train or allocate some minor work to Victor.

However, Victor starts to learn by observation. Most of the knowledge he gains is through his own efforts. He has understood the value of learning through observation. He used to listen to senior talking over the phone, responding to customers and bosses queries, he learns from it.

Victor speaks to himself "I will get an opportunity to learn from him, he is too busy these days..." He sits idle for almost two weeks now.

After they reach home four of the roommates discuss their day's experience. Everyone experiences the same.

One day in the office, he overhears the discussion between his senior and his manager. They are discussing department's performance.

Manager, "Top Management is concerned, customers are complaining that we do not close the assignments on time. You can understand that our clients give us business and any impact on their work adversely affects our business. Customers are our number one priority."

Senior, "Yes Sir, I am fully focused on the tasks and trust me I give more than hundred percent to meet requirements, but what to do sir, I am overloaded and even if I take all necessary actions on time, the list of action items is endless and some projects delay; quality gets a hit."

Manager, "We have recently given you a new resource, what's his name, hmm... Victor."

Victor attentively listens after they quote his name, there is some discussion about him, something imperative.

Senior grumbles, "Sir, please try to understand, I just told you about my overload and training a new resource consumes additional time. Customer satisfaction level already dipping, will drop further, there will be more escalations and further impact our business."

Manager, "I understand this point, I too had recommended top management to hire experienced resources.

You know that experienced resources come at a higher cost. However, the goal of our company is to reduce cost. Remember if the quality of work continuously deteriorates, we might lose a few customers and jobs too, include yours and mine.

Training him might take your time initially, but later on, the advantage is on your side. You must recall your days when you had started as a new employee. Today, you are an invaluable asset to the company and any impact on you would be detrimental to your family. Hope you get my message."

Senior, "Yes, I got your message. I hope you take a note to the consequences and will be ready to handle the complaints you are going to receive."

This response frustrates the manager, he harshly replies,

"Look, as I said earlier, I need results. I can give you a good piece of advice, cut the time you spend on smoking, taking leisure walks post lunch. Stop to criticize company and people in your free time. I am your manager, and I know how much time you spend on what, stop scrolling up and down on your computer screen to show yourself busy. I was in that position previous to you, and I know what can be done. If I had not trained you well, you would not have been handling this position at this moment, and I would have not also reached the management level.

You remember Tom and Rohn, who did not take an interest in developing the provided resources. As a consequence, the performance dropped significantly, and they were fired. I hope you do not want to be one of those. I would review the situation regularly, and if you do not improve, prepare yourself for the aftermaths.

I repeat, if you do not change, you will be changed.

No more questions, you can go now." He almost yells at the senior.

Victor speaks to himself, "After hearing the discussion it does not seem that paucity of time is the real issue." He is sitting idle for almost two weeks after hiring. When the senior comes back from the room, he looks with fiery eyes and tells Victor, "You need to sit with me after office hours, I will train you on how to handle the work and assist me in future."

"Sure Sir," acknowledges Victor.

Senior re-warns, "After office hours means, strictly after office hours." Victor nods again.

The senior does not turn as bad as a person, he has fears to lose his prominence in office. But his manager's stern threat overshadows his insecurity. The training which he imparts is an outcome of the push from his manager.

Victor recalls Patrick and Colonel David Barr,

Some people help selflessly and there are others who are overloaded and do not wish to share the loads.

When the senior starts with the first session of download, he gets a surprise that Victor is not as naive as he had perceived. He senses his eagerness to learn and becomes aware that he has already acquired a good sense of work on his own. However, instead of being comfortable with this revelation, he feels more insecure. He cannot imagine a new employee to succeed or supersede him.

We need to remember, leadership is not driven by the feeling of insecurity but by the sense of coaching and turning others into leaders. A lot of people have this mentality in office, they sit on the knowledge and information like a snake is guarding treasure. Make sure you are not one of them.

Victor makes meticulous efforts and learns work quickly, he is now "On his marks; Ready to Get, Set, and Go."

"If you pick the right people and give them the opportunity to spread their wings—and put compensation as a carrier behind it—you almost do not have to manage them." – Jack Welch

Till present times, Victor remembers and applies this principle in his life:

To succeed in life, he creates and trains his people to be more successful. As a result he leads a team with high intelligence, skill sets, and a contagious attitude. A team whose attributes succeed in all he undertakes. The team members have the ability to change the results through their skills.

Chapter – 8

"Desired Personality Concept- How to be one."

The Vampire of a Weak Personality

"It is wonderful to have someone praise you, to be desired."

-Marilyn Monroe

In a short span of time, Victor starts to work independently. He reaches office early, checks the list of open tasks, organize the work and execute.

He remembered the story of a farmer which his father used to tell him,

"Remain in Shade, My Son"

"There was a farmer, who used to live with his three sons in a village. The farmer was very hard working, one day he fell sick. Uncertain of his future, he called his sons and told them, I give land near the river, to eldest son, land near the village border to middle son and land near the spring to the youngest son. Please take care of your fields and the crops will take care of you for rest of the year. Remember my sons, always go in shade and come back in the shade. All three sons started to cultivate their lands. Eldest son and youngest son had nothing to worry about their fields, they became lazy. However, the middle son who got the land near the outskirts truly followed his father's instruction, he used to go to the fields always before sunrise and came back after sunset, thus always remained in the shade. He worked hard continuously on fields, he had put more efforts than any other. The reaping season began, other two sons noticed that birds and stray animals destroyed a significant portion of their fields. Middle son had the best harvest."

Moral: Adding extra, converts ordinary to extraordinary. Just add, a bit extra effort in each work you do, even a little will make your outcomes astonishing.

Victor follows the moral of the story. As of yet, his efforts remain invisible to the top management and he understands it is very early to expect this.

He needs to be a more desirable person for the company.

This dream to be a desirable person brings him to the term 'desired personality' and which later on develops into 'Desired Personality Concept – How to be one.'

He continues to note learnings in the notebook, he wants to make a difference.

"Commitment to yourself - I will make a difference and make consistent efforts."

Victor shows good results at his work and he always dresses well. However, he feels that 'something' lacks in the quest to be a more desirable person. He also notices that all people in preparation for the day, wear good clothes, and prepare themselves well. However, when they reach in public, all of them turn into an unnoticeable crowd. Why does it happen? He does not remember many faces that cross him on the regular way. He notices only a few people who are physically attractive, but he discounts it as God's gift. What is the 'X' factor in this?

He thinks often, and arrives at a conclusion "If I work well, dress well and also deliver consistent results, I will become more desirable, someday, maybe it's only a pursuit of persistence and time."

But, he is not sure if it is the right assumption.

Alas! Patrick or Colonel are not here to guide him so, he takes his notebook out.

Victor looks at the notes and recites aloud,

"Usage of knowledge has become shallow, knowledge is spread like rainwater, which dries up within a few hours or a day. The knowledge needs to be in depth like an ocean, and we must know how to apply and use it."

This postulation triggers him to think more deeply, and he suspects, "No, it's not purely about being well dressed, working good or tenure. My senior is working for a long time, he delivers the results, he dresses well too, but I do not think it makes him any desirable. There certainly is something additional to these factors. But what is it, which value is missing?"

Victor does not arrive at a conclusion that night. He sleeps over it to come up with a better outcome. He thinks, thinks and thinks more……..

He visualizes all phases of his life and goes through each and every event thoughtfully. He questions himself, "Who are the people whom I adore in my life?"

He counts on fingers, "Patrick, Colonel, Mother, Sister and Brother, Childhood Friend, Neighbor, Classmate, College Professor, Manager, and Colleagues." These were the people he believed are most desirable in his life. He has the list available now.

To understand this concept, readers can also prepare the list of people they feel are desirable in their life. The desired personality concept applies equally to all aspects of life whether personal or professional. Everyone has a different set of desired people in life.

"But what after this?" Victor thinks "Now, I have the list of desired people but what do I do with this?"

All people were different, unlike traits, dissimilar relationship and unique times of their appearance in his life. A few were from his birth and few were most recent. Apart from a few instances, he could not even remember how they dressed. He could also relate that all of them were not from his work sphere.

It reaffirms that it is not merely about time, dress and working well or get results.

He further expands the list to inspirational people and entrepreneurs who he admires.

"I need to go deeper than surface level, find reasons why I like them, perhaps that is going to give me the answers for a 'Desired Personality Concept- How to be one' he ponders.

So he deep dives, stacks the list further in four groups, Victor finds that not everyone has the matching qualities:

Group A – Mother, Sister, Brother, and Friends and their qualities,

"Never above you. Never below you. Always beside you."-Walter Winchell

Compassion/Care – They care for me, put themselves in my shoes and feel for me. Their care is not dependent on self-interest. Their interests are not monetary and they are there with me through thick and thin. The feeling that they think about me is the most valuable part of my life. Whenever I feel low, I think about them which fills me with energy and vigor. Parents bear the work stress to take care of kids. Wife wakes up two hours early to ensure that her husband and children reach office and school on time. She waits in the evening to serve them coffee when they get back home.

"Never believe that a few caring people cannot change the world. For, indeed, that's all who ever have."

- Margaret Mead

Trust – They believe in me and have faith in my abilities. They believe that I can succeed even before I have produced any results. They believe in my potential and encourage me. The most significant characteristic of trust is to place self-reliance in others, to share a top-secret and be confident that they will not disclose it. Trust is essential, because we all have things we need to talk about that we do not want to share with others.

"If you can trust, something or other will always happen and will help your growth. You will be provided for. Whatsoever is needed at a particular time will be given to you, never before it. You get it only when you need it, and there is not even a single moment's delay. When you need it you get it, immediately, instantly! That's the beauty of trust. By and by you learn the ways of how existence goes on providing for you, how existence goes on caring about you. You are not living in an indifferent

existence. It does not ignore you. You are unnecessarily worried; all is provided for. Once you have learnt the knack of trust, all worry disappears."- Osho

Dependability – They depend on me, and I too can count on them. Not only they stand with me through thick and thin, but also in happiness. These are the people I want to be successful for and share my proceeds with. Our life is to live our promises and walk the talk, it is a fundamental requirement for collaboration, and it allows people to work together, perceive that friends, family, and peers take care of responsibilities assigned to them. Machines prove more reliable than men, that is why those substitute them. If you are reliable you erase, confusion, doubts, failures and almost every reason of being unsuccessful.

Dependability lets us sleep peacefully at home when there is a war on the border. It helps billionaires build their success upon. Without dependability, no one can succeed as no one can be omnipresent to handle the size of the dreams they have. Be dependable, be trustworthy and be consistent.

Forgiveness/Tolerance – They forgive, tolerate my mistakes and do not throw me out of their lives because of my inadvertent errors. They guide me accurate and give me an opportunity to correct my mistakes.

Love – Their love is unconditional which makes them walk miles entirely to see me and they feel the agony when I am in pain. They wish to take my pains and think more about my well-being than I do. They see a nightmare and wake up at midnight to check if everything is perfect, they use my name as a secret password for their systems. They are the people who make my life worth living.

"Love is patient, love is kind. It does not envy, it does not boast, it is not proud. It is not rude, it is not self-seeking, it is not easily angered, it keeps no record of wrongs. Love does not delight in evil but rejoices with the truth. It always protects, always trusts, always hopes, it always preserves". (1 Corinthians 13:1)

Group B – Manager, Colleagues

"A good manager finds satisfaction in helping others be productive, not being the most productive person in the room."- Paul Glen

Decisiveness – They make faster decisions and honor timelines linked to the goals and have a sense of urgency. They evaluate and analyze the decisions before, which shows the amount of critical thinking they undergo. The fortune of an organization can change by the influence of the decisions. Slower decisions can result disastrous, Doctors make quick decisions about the operation of their patients, and this is the margin between life and death here. Faster decisions never impact any person adversely, people who are fast and decisive can quickly change the course of the life for better. As an example, mass manufacturing decisions produce a large volume of products, which in turn improves the prosperity of a company and the country. When experience and a decent rationale backs decisions, they help us to win.

Team Spirit – The ones who work and run like a baton race team, inform the next person to succeed and win. The contribution of each individual is a key success factor for a relationship, family, organization, and nation. Teamwork applies in all phases of life, most of the times, a task involves more than one person, and the outcomes can only be positive if we apply teamwork. For example, marriage becomes successful when husband and wife work together as a team. A student becomes successful when teachers, parents and student work as a unit. A business succeeds when all its members work as one. To win or to lose is the margin between a good and bad teamwork.

Honesty/Fairness - They perform their duties honestly and fairly treat others. If the parents are honest, their children would be honest and disciplined in life. They groom them in a realistic environment, and their children turn out as good citizens. They display honesty in every sphere of life. You can trust the honest people to handle bigger responsibilities. As a bulb lights up the world, an honest person illuminates a life, honesty creates trust, and generates respect. Most of the countries do not develop as the leaders are dishonest, and they do so for their personal gains. This deprived leadership keeps the countries poor, makes it difficult to do business, opportunities do not create for the youths. The younger generation in these countries is increasingly turning into criminals. Without honesty, their future will be even worse.

Applied Knowledge – They develop necessary skills and learn new things, they are adaptable to change. The difference in applied knowledge and knowledge is enormous. If knowledge does not provide solutions for your challenges, it is not worth. Applied knowledge is the vital power which makes you successful, unless we implement it, we cannot expect to get results, more than making things happen, we wait for the things to happen on their own. Applied knowledge is when faith realizes into opportunities and makes you succeed.

Leadership – People lead because the way they carry themselves is adorable. They are approachable, confident and committed. Their leadership inspires people, makes teams believe in them and move single-mindedly in one direction. Leadership is the quality which frees the nations from foreign rules. Leaders travel across the world to motivate people, they empower people irrespective of the geographical and political restrictions. The history has witnessed that the success or failure of a country is the difference between its good and bad leadership. Leaders are the hope when there is no hope, and they are the promise for a better future. Our real heroes are the leaders who can help us achieve success, people who take others with them.

"An employee made a mistake that cost the company $10 million, he walked into the office of Tom Watson, the C.E.O., expecting to get fired. "Fire you?" Mr. Watson asked. "I just spent $10 million educating you." — Adam Grant

Group C - College Professor, School Teachers, Mentors

"A mentor empowers a person to see a possible future, and believes it can be obtained.'" — Shawn Hitchcock

Consistent Learners — They are avid readers and consistently update themselves. They learn for self-enlightenment and from all others. Learning helps explore new opportunities for the individuals and sequels in continuous improvements, erases thoughts which do not work and replace with the new ideas. The individuals who are not steady learners are like obsolete models which no one likes to own. To upgrade yourself is a continuous process which in turn increases your value every single day. The day you miss to learn new is the day you devalue yourself. If you devalue yourself, do not expect the world to value you. Knowledge is all around, and unless we learn and apply new things, our life becomes stagnant, we wonder to figure out what is wrong. Be a consistent learner and make mindful efforts.

Mentors – They mentor and contribute to the improvement of society. They educate, instruct which in turn inspires others to reach greater heights. They bring incomparable value to the lives of people. A mentor brings out the diamond out of you, they cut, polish and make your worth visible to the world. While the whole world ignores your potential, they work on your day and night, not only in your presence but also in absence. When you are busy to make a living, they create plans to make you a fortune. They guide you, challenge your limitations, and break your myths to bring the best out of you. Not only they make you realize your powers but also prove it through your success as evidence.

Engagement – They engage themselves and involve others in productive tasks. While most of the people do not care, they alter your life for better by engaging in your interests. They engage to bring your ideas to action. You get a marvelous benefit out of it and develop a broader range of skills. Most prominently, you prepare yourself to make a difference, for all around you. Engagement empowers you to create a difference. The outcomes for communities and organizations vary by the level of constructive engagements they have within.

Reviewers – Because they are consistent learners, mentors and engage in you, they review, inspect, introspect and provide feedbacks for further improvements. They figure out the factors which lead to your struggle and cause a failure, they fine tune the approach and redo it until it works in your favor. Having an honest review is the best way to come out of flaws.

Communicators – They communicate relevant messages from the books and their own experiences, this helps us to understand our lives better. Otherwise, no one will ever take the pain to go through those in-depth messages. Their purpose of their communication is to bestow the knowledge which you may apply in practical life, and they give this in advance. It is the eminence of a learner to use the knowledge which mentors have communicated. You need to make use of it and share to the people for the welfare of society.

Group D – Entrepreneurs, Inspirational People

'I failed in some subjects in exam, but my friend passed in all. Now he is an engineer in Microsoft and I am the owner of Microsoft.' – Bill Gates

Optimism – They are always optimistic and trust that tasks can be done. They think out of the box. Optimism is an attitude that focuses on what is worthy about our current situation and the forthcoming. Everything that is attractive or enchanting in this world comes with agony and loss; optimism is a mindful discriminatory concentration for a worthy cause.

Optimism gives us vigor; it makes our struggles lighter. In the end, it makes us believe that even though some of our labors will fail, others will flourish, and we cannot know in advance what will fail and what will work. When we are optimistic we are cheerful, and make others happy. Being an optimist is the best favor a person can do to the environment and himself. It is not dependent on external scenarios, it is what you generate within. Always be mindful and make conscious efforts to remain an optimist, whatever situation may arise, if you are sanguine, you are a winner. Optimism has always changed the directions of the world in many ways, refer Olympians or scientists who never give up. Be optimistic, reflect optimism.

Originality – They develop and enable existing concepts in a different way. They take it to large scale and the benefits spread across the boundaries. Originality rules the world, if you talk about, Thomas Alva Edison or Steve Jobs, they had one attribute in common, originality. Today we see light bulb kills the vampire of darkness, and life feels impossible without it. Someone discovered CFL and LED to improve on that originality. From aircraft to rockets and spaceships everything is either original or innovation. India has their satellites on

Mars because of originality that too at one tenth of the cost NASA spent on their mission. If they had replicated or bought the concept from NASA their cost would have been way higher.

Visionary – Their vision is to look into the future and explore the unexplored. They make dreams turn into reality, with hard work, persistence and high levels of confidence. Napoleon was known as a stupendous political leader, he did many things for his people, and even for the countries he had conquered. His legal systems are still relevant. Visionary leaders changed the systems, they allowed all men to vote, irrespective of creed or affluence, ended slavery. They built roads, gardens, reservoirs, and other public conveniences. They created the Banks, which permitted people to become richer. Old time entrepreneurs exhausted resources with their extravagant lifestyle, while visionary leaders raised the standard of living for the entire mankind. To them everything begins with a dream to do better.

Risk Taking – They put everything into the ventures they undertake and carry all financial risks. However when they reap the benefits of risks, they distribute it across associated people. They create opportunities and provide employment to others. Individuals do not advance if they do not follow the technique to alter the old and try new. Columbus tried to reach India via a new route and he discovered America. If he had taken the conventional route as other sailors, he could never have achieved this mind-boggling success. Nowadays, we see gadgets and other developments which help to raise the standard of living. Scientists and investigators use different ways to do things and methods which open the new possibilities in ordinary lives.

Self-Belief – They are self-believers even when the world is against their initiatives. Their strong belief helps them to sail through the ocean of external doubts. They stand for themselves when no one takes a stand for them. Self-confidence is developed and it cannot be imparted. It is up to the person to determine how much belief they can create within. You must first have faith in yourself prior to others can trust you. It is a natural spirit that comes along as we advance in emotions, materials, enthusiasm and spirituality. Self-belief is the testimony that you will act in an adequate and efficient way.

Opportunity/Chances – Whereas ordinary person waits for opportunities, they create opportunities for themselves and others. Take your chances and if you turn out to be successful, you may be able to alter the way the world operates. So many opportunities arrive, but we stay incognizant. We suffer or regret whole life as an outcome. Here is a story:

God and the Fool

A few travelers were cruising on a ship. The ship got hit by a storm and was about to drown. They were praying to the God to save their lives. Lifeguards rescued a few and a few others were taken away by a nearby ship. All the travelers but one survived as they took their chance in some manner. One of the travelers could not be saved as he did not accept the opportunity given to him, he wanted God to appear and protect him. After Death he went to heaven and asked God, why he was not saved from death, he had his family waiting at home. The God responded: 'I gave you three chances, first with the ability to swim, second to shout for a lifeguard, third through a ship, but you overlooked, thinking that I will come to save you. I gave you a life full of far-sightedness, knowledge, astuteness and bravery, you never used those qualities and missed the opportunities.

After Victor defines the list of qualities, another question struck in his mind "Do I have any of these qualities, for which I appreciate them."

"Wow! That is a wide list of qualities, how can I have all of them in me? Ok, let me not think to acquire all of these at one go. Let me make a sincere effort to at least add a few."

He takes a few steps at a time, if not a few, start with one step.

Victor is in the process to discover himself. He remembers that his current personality is a consequence of a difficult childhood which had stopped him from developing fully. Earlier, he had no interests or ambitions, even his relocation to this city was forced by an unfortunate incident.

He knows that he like these people, for their qualities. He feels fortunate to have navigators to show the right direction. He finds that his life has affected positively by the influence of Patrick and Colonel. He gets a sense of clarity, confidence and positivity.

A few people have a significant effect on our life, the people who have a proven record of greatness, simply to hear their stories can turn lives into fortune without even seeing or meeting them. Inside, we all know the people we adore, we need to focus on the qualities what they have and try to imbibe those qualities within us. We know what we want. Take actions to convert the desire into demand, once it's converted into a demand (ability to pay the price), it automatically converts into a command (we own it).

Victor takes a practical approach, he selects five qualities to proceed with – Dependability, Team Spirit, Knowledge, Communication, and Vision. He knows that if he starts with all qualities at a time, it would be too much for him. He begins to work on these, and the effects soon reflect in his performance. All customers and team members start to appreciate his attitude, communication style and delivery commitment.

He gets more responsibilities and after one and a half year, his senior's manager, who was happy with the upshots, spots his potential. The good words reach to the top management, and they want to see him. He will meet the company Managing Director, **Robin Steve**, the founder and owner of the company. Who has been awarded The Best Entrepreneur of The Year, had diversified businesses, and his net worth was close to a billion.

His meeting gets scheduled for next week. Victor prepares himself for the meeting. He had made it a point to take notes and refresh them weekly. He used to capture all new ideas which he felt would be helpful in his notebook.

The will to win, the desire to succeed, the urge to reach your full potential... these are the keys that will unlock the door to personal excellence. -Confucius

Chapter – 9

"Communicate for Opportunities Concept – Meeting Robin Steve"

The Vampire of Weak Communication

"Take advantage of every opportunity to practice your communication skills so that when important occasions arise, you will have the gift, the style, the sharpness, the clarity, and the emotions to affect other people."- Jim Rohn

The day arrives, Victor sets to meet Robin Steve. In past few months apart from his daily chores, he had been working on "Desired Personality Concept- How to be one". He had judiciously worked on Dependability, Team Spirit, Knowledge, Communication, and Vision.

Robin is not in his chamber. His secretary advises him to wait inside the cabin and that Robin will join any moment. When Vick enters the chamber, he notes that apart from the arresting library in the room, multiple business awards festooned the wall. "The Best Entrepreneur of The Year" award shines.

It is a hot topic of discussion among the business community and media these days, he links.

Victor makes himself comfortable on the chair and wits, "What I need to do to become one among these entrepreneurs, who are highly respected, live a wonderful life and create opportunities for others?"

He harks back to a Jesse Owens quote, "We all have dreams. But in order to make dreams come into reality, it takes an awful lot of determination, dedication, self-discipline, and effort."

Before he delves more on this, he hears the sound of the door opening. He stands from his chair to greet Robin Steve. Victor had read his stories in the newspapers and heard about him from peers. Personally, he never had an opportunity to meet him, and he had just glimpsed him on the floor a few times.

"Hey, Victor, how are you doing?" – Asks Robin and quickly sits on the chair.

Robin is a dynamic person in his early forties, and certainly he looks younger than his age. He is a self-made man, and currently his stories are told across the country.

"Good Morning Robin. I am doing well."

Robin is in a fun mood, Victor assumes it is his nature to drive a large enterprise with fun, wit and skillful financial and business acumen.

He wants to check the confidence level of Victor. So in response to his greetings he poses an abrupt question back,

"What's good about this morning Victor? Can you be more specific?"

Nobody had replied to a 'good morning' like this in the past, Victor has an entirely new situation. He disallows the vampire of weak communication to masticate as he does not desire to lose a chance to create a good first impression.

"Well Sir, it's a sunny day, birds are singing outside, our company's results are beyond market's expectations. I am meeting with you for the first time, and we are going to discuss business." Victor stops for a while and asks, "There are other things too Robin if you will like to know more."

Robin smiles, no one had replied to a sudden stupid question like this so far.

He notices Victor's intelligence and promptness but, tests him more, "Yes, tell me more, I am curious."

Victor Continues, "We won a substantial order from an automotive giant, which begins a new era in our company, everyone in the company is happy and geared up to deliver nothing less than the best. All of this happened today morning."

Robin spontaneously laughs, "It is good to see your gusto and positive attitude. It's more important to have the presence of mind than just physical presence. I like it!

Ok, Victor can I call you Vick?" Vick Okays

"So Vick, you may not be aware, why I have called you. We have an opening and we are considering you to lead your function. Your manager will leave to pursue a better opportunity outside the organization.

When I asked him he suggested considering an internal replacement. He was convinced that we have a talent available within our company and he had identified a person who could replace him." Robin continues further,

"To my surprise, his recommendation was not someone up in the hierarchy, rather he recommended you. I shared my concerns that you are too immature to handle a role of this magnitude and also that being so young, people might not accept you as a leader. But he insisted that you must be given this opportunity despite a couple of years' experience in the company."

I checked with a few others and our customers for a second opinion, and they too confirmed this as the best choice. "Tell me how you built such high, relationship with all of them?"

It astonishes Victor, he had no guestimate for the reasons behind this meeting.

If he passes this test, it will be a life-changing bargain for him. Victor responds,

"Relationships in business are dependent on the quality of work we deliver and the way we make users feel while we provide it.

There are six simple rules which I always follow to create a strong customer relationship:

1.   **Call my customers before they call me**: I do it not only to update on the progress but also to assure that we care about them. It sends an indirect message that we are compassionate about their requirements, and we address those with the required focus. I practice the same with my family and friends as well.

2.   **Actions:** In addition to the updates, I make them aware of additional actions which are in place to suffice the requirements and the business continuity plan if, the early actions miss the mark. It asserts that everything is under control and we have plans to handle contingencies.

3.   The importance of complete picture: I firmly believe, the work and customers that I handle are of paramount importance, and they are an integral element of an end to end value chain. If I handle an assignment of Pharmaceutical manufacturer, I know this is important as production lines run on the supplies, and any delay can result in a line stoppage. This break leads to losses to the company, which culminates in job and credibility loss. The patients wait for those medicines in hospitals, and any time loss adversely impacts their wellbeing. I take responsibility and make every possible effort to forbid any such impact.

4.   Consistent – When I follow this I make sure that I am consistent, every fraction of a second. If I am inconsistent, the effects do not endure, customers remain full of predicament whether to trust or not trust my words, when to trust and when not. Consistency makes me more reliable.

5.   Experience: I always remain humble to deliver a pleasurable experience. It's not worth if we provide and perform our duties with a bad experience to the customers. Similarly, I treat my peers and colleagues with respect and dignity, when they walk, or I walk to them for any assistance.

6. **No criticism in absence:** I do not criticize anyone in absence. I believe that any issues with a person can improve by an open conversation. The disagreements which we cannot mention in a person's presence must not be proclaimed in his absence. This ends the tradition to pass blames on the people who are absent or have left the organization

Victor stops for a while.

Robin listens to him patiently and thinks that Victor of course is wiser than his assumptions. Now he knows the reason why the manager, customers, and peers were so confident in him.

He has a superb clarity, not only he executes but also he is aware of his actions and impacts. Most of the people go with the flow, they deliver but are unaware of the value and purpose of their actions. This boy is different, but he is still too young for this level of responsibility.

Victor closes, "This is what I believe, and it inspires me. This is how I am able to build robust and reliable relationships in such a short period. I am honest in every aspect."

Robin's eyes shrink, he asks further to clear his doubt,

"Victor, I appreciate your answers; sensible and precise. But do not you think you are too young to handle this role, there are people in the team who have been with the company over a decade, and they may not take it well?

As an individual contributor you are accountable for independent work but when you become a manager, your success depends on the way your team delivers, they might not like you to lead because of your age."

Victor thinks for a moment, he knows that it is a valid concern, however, what he communicates might convince Robin. It's all about creating trust through communication. What you communicate under which scenarios creates a path of your life.

"Robin your concern is correct, and I acknowledge that."

It tests Victor's confidence and ability to perform under pressure. The people who are not confident quit easily when a challenging scenario arrives, they run even earlier than entering the real situation. Only an individual with strong self-belief can pass the test.

Robin ponders, "Let me see how the boy comes up with an answer, is he going to make or give it up?"

"Robin, I understand your point well. It would be a challenging situation, but the outcome of this action would depend on my efforts. When I talk about the discomfort of seniors, I need to make sure either my words or my actions do not hurt them. Instead, I intend to win respect with my deeds and humility toward them. I need to communicate myself positively that, I can work out this. Unless I am confident, I would not be able to make them comfortable.

Age is just a mental stage, it is more psychological. People at twenty can feel like eighty and vice versa. This is dependent on what their mind has exposed to.

Young age is not a concern Robin, as per the best of my knowledge, you started quite young with no support of family or financial institutions. They backed you only once you had proved your worthiness. Warren Buffet started at the age of eleven, people laughed, and today he is the most successful investor in the world."

In the meantime, Robin assesses the research work Victor has done on him and the life of other successful people. He himself was inspired by the success stories of others. But not so easy, there would be something I can catch Victor on, he wants to make sure that he is making a right decision, and all questions have to be asked now itself.

Robin grills further, "What does that mean, are you saying that older people are not good, are they waste?"

"No Robin, I have never mentioned that, their experience and wisdom are the guiding light for the young. What I mean is, age is a mental stage, and it is more psychological than physical. Let me elaborate by quoting Jonathan Mendes, at the age ninety-six he set the record of the eldest finisher in the New York City Marathon's history. As a Marine Colonel Jonathan Mendes flew hundred plus operations in the World War II and then more than seventy assignments in the Korean War. He trained John Glenn and Ted Williams. He still walks two miles every day. There can be, no better example. Today his story is a source of inspiration to many." Victor Stops.

Robin takes no more time and concludes, "Vick, I am confident that you are the right person to lead the function. The responsibilities are high, and some exposures will be totally new. You need to make sure that whatever you claimed today, you will always follow that. The expectations are high, and you should meet or exceed those."

Victor feels happy as he has communicated skillfully. His heart thanks Patrick, Colonel, and his manager for their guidance and support. It had never happened in the past, no employee had got promoted like that.

He is aware that now, he needs to be more sensitive to new requirements. He goes home, takes a few notes and sleeps calmly. Jim Rohn had figured it out "If you just communicate, you can get by. But if you communicate skillfully, you can work miracles."

Chapter – 10

"Decision Making – The Right Way"

The Vampire of indecisiveness

"Whenever you're making an important decision, first ask if it gets you closer to your goals or farther away. If the answer is closer, pull the trigger. If it's farther away, make a different choice. Conscious choice making is a critical step in making your dreams a reality."

- *Jillian Michaels*

Victor increases his efforts, he comes earlier and leaves last. He does an excellent job, except his senior, everyone else is happy with him. The senior does not come to terms with Victor's success, he leaves the job. Victor ends up one resource less and the workload increases. He works harder, and the team members support him to their level best. Victor feels the pressure to complete tasks, However, he does not approach Robin for replacement of resource.

He discusses it with a close friend, who suggests that he is new to the role and if he raises this issue with Robin, it may not reflect well on his leadership abilities, so he needs to manage the problem on his own.

Although the team stretches their work hours, they feel exultant under his encouragement, they have no customer complaints and most importantly, results are great.

One day, two of his team members meet with a serious accident, they land in the hospital and put on bed rest for a couple of weeks. Victor already had tremendous pressure, he keeps his friend's advice in mind and puts even more hours at work, sometimes sleeps in office at his desk. His friend reassures and encourages him, not to worry as the two employees would be will in a month's time.

With his core strength, Victor takes all pressures, he wants to show a difference. He decides not to contact Robin as he was traveling. Vampire of over commitment struck.

However, during this time, one of the assignments delays, and a stern complaint directly reaches Robin. When Robin comes back, he calls Victor to understand what has gone wrong.

Patiently, he hears Victor and points out,

"Victor you should have called me. Do you think I do not know that one person alone is incapable to take a load of four? I would have shifted resources from other departments to support you. It was an easy decision.

You need to assess the gravity of a situation and make decisions.

Now you have a more responsible role, and decision making is an integral element of it. I think you need some help with it. I will give you some guidance on "Right Decision Making" which will help you to be successful in your job and life."

"Vick, there is a team which reports to you, and you are accountable for the decisions of your department.

You are a key determiner in building company rapport across businesses and clients. As I had assured earlier, I have confidence in you.

So far you have followed decisions, now you are required to decide on your own. What you decide, your team has to follow. I know this is a new kind of experience for you. Many superb individual contributors fail when put into team leader's role.

To prepare and make you successful in your new role, I am sharing some fundamentals on 'Decision Making – The Right Way' with you."

"Your success is my success, and every employee's success is company's success."

Victor thinks, how different it is at the top? Owners want all employees to be successful because their business success builds on each individual success. They take risks, pay them and generate revenue. When, the same owner divides the roles, into different functions, teams start to work in silos and create the walls. They pull other functions down as if they pull down competitors. The primary reasons are insecurity, fear, and loss of importance. At the top level, there is no inward insecurity and fear. There is only one will, will to succeed.

He makes a point to write it in his notebook when back home.

Robin turns toward Vick and continues,

"You know how people decide, Mahatma Gandhi decided when he was thrown off a train at Pietermaritzburg after he had declined to move from the first-class. It was the moment of decision which quaked the entire world.

Back to India, he had decided to throw British Empire out. He had no weapons or treasures to fight such mighty empire, so he took the path of non-violence. "Satyagraha" which means "insistence on truth." He decided to recycle the weakness of masses into a strong weapon, started nonviolent movements one after other, the entire nation came together and killed the vampire of foreign servitude. He had zero resources but the consummate strategy. In all stages of our life, we need to make decisions, immense and trivial."

"Vick, what do you think, when do we grow up? We become adults at the age of eighteen years, but when do we actually grow up?"

Victor judges, "Sorry Robin, I am not sure on your question? Going by the topic under discussion, I believe growing up has something in common with decision making."

"Yes Vick, you have got your brain in gear now.

We grow up when we start to take our own decisions. Decision making is the point of convergence for work, life and success. It is predominantly important when your decisions also impact others.

Till the time we look at our parents, teachers, friends and managers for decision making, we are grown in age but not mentally.

Do you still need to hold fingers of your mother to walk?

Do you still need your teachers to tell you, how to read, A to Z?

No, Why? Because you have already learned it, and you can do it yourself. Then why do we still need someone to make a decision for us? We must learn, how to make decisions, the right way.

Tomorrow as a leader, you will have to take a lot of decisions and you need to prepare for that.

OK tell me Vick, when you are stuck in a difficult situation, whose help do you take to decide?"

Victor replies, "I discuss with my best friend. He is a superb childhood friend and is always there to support me."

Robin had expected a similar answer, he confirms, "That's true in most stressful situations, normal people turn to their friends for help on decision making. That's common.

By the way, what is the age of your best friend Vick?"

"He is almost my age, we have played together. The difference in our age, would not be, more than six months."

Robin, "Vick, tell me, he is your age, your qualifications and experience are also probably equivalent to him. Whatever he can think, you can also think. Am I correct?"

Victor – "Yes Robin, that's what I told. Whenever I go to him and discuss my problem, once he confirms the solution, only then we finalize the decision."

Robin –"That is a wrong way to make a decision, Vick. You do not go to your friend to make a right decision but, to confirm the possible decision you have already assumed. As he is your buddy, he confirms the decision. Now you have got two votes for barking up the wrong tree. Please remember, even if both of you agree to a wrong decision does not make it right.

And this is funny, that whoever friend we go for advice, he suggests a solution. Practically, no one has all expertise to advice on all matters. Their advice is as useful as a chocolate teapot.

Instead, you should go to a person or consultant experienced in that field. Specialists who have relevant experience to handle such situation will be able to guide you better."

"No one has explained it to me in this way Robin. I acknowledge that I used to discuss most of the difficult situations with my friend only because I knew he would agree with my opinion. I had not even discussed with my mother, who was more experienced as I was afraid that she wouldn't approve it.

That's why I used to get into a problem after some time, I can connect it. I was in reality not looking for right decisions but more for an accord to do what I had in my mind.

I get the message - Always seek advice from, experienced people and experts of the related field, to make a decision. That is the right way of making decisions."

Robin is happy that Victor has realized the importance of the point, he reaffirms,

"You are on the right track now, Vick, nothing benefits than taking advice from right people. In business most of the people charge money for advice, the eminence of good advice is so significant that it has turned into a massive industry."

Victor nods, Robin continues,

"This is the fundamental of any decision making, which you need to keep in mind.

This is THUMB RULE NO 1 of the right way of making decisions.

Now we come back to other aspects of decision making. In life, we have to take decisions in five major areas

1. Business – Products, career, strategic and tactical decisions

2. Relationship – Compatibility, Engagement, Time, Care

3. Health – Fitness, Exercise, Schedules, Consistency, Diet

4. Finance- Sourcing, selling, margins

5. Academics – courses, specializations, basics

Robin explains further, "As we are in business I will concentrate on, "Right Way of Making Business Decisions".

Remember, wrong decisions may result in bankruptcy, partnership split, individual's failure and noncooperation.

The complexity level of all decisions, does not take it to the level of external consultants. You need to develop your own skills to test that decisions are made in the right way. Always follow below six qualification benchmarks:

Headline Test

Always weigh 'What will be the impact of your decision if it makes to the headline of tomorrow's newspaper'. Will it make you feel proud, good, bad or ugly? It's important to visualize final outcome in advance to any decision. Take the decisions which pass the Headline Test.

Clarity

Decisions must be clear enough. While it cascades through the various level of management, a decision must not lose its clarity. Lack of transparency not only disturbs the quality of decision-making but also slows down the whole course of implementation. Remember without clarity ships do not sail, aircrafts do not take off.

Practicality

Decisions must be practical. Practicality makes plans ready for implementation. People understand through practical ways better, rather than textbooks and theories.

Well Analyzed

Before you finalize any decision, make sure that it has gone through necessary tools of validation, like data analysis and brainstorming. Make sure it is visible to and accepted by the key stakeholders in the organization. It will test the strength and weakness of a decision and make it better. It is easy to build a new structure rather renovate an old one. Same applies to the decision-making process as well.

Fast and Timely

Today is the time of high speed and high-end technology. With accuracy industry needs, timeliness and speed. Decisions must be faster to support execution of strategy and operations. They must not sleep on manager's desk. If decisions delay, not only the projects, but also the time to implement plan B misses.

Fine Tune

Once you have applied the decisions, go back and fine tune it. We learn a lot of things post implementation. Fine tune, improve and move ahead."

While Robin explains, Victor takes notes consistently, he knows that he has introduced to a new concept, which will prove of surprising worth if applied correctly. He also could correlate why Patrick had told him that he would learn decision making under practical scenarios. Once you enter in the real situation, you know the importance.

"You are the same today that you are going to be five years from now except for two things: the people with whom you associate and the books you read."

— Charles Jones

Victor had started as a poor guy, surrounded by all sort of bad attitudes, scarcities but he turned it to prominence, you too can kill these vampires.

We need a paradigm shift in our mind. Whatever we have learned in school, this is the time to put that into the application. Start thinking right, doing right. If you are in school, learn to change your habit from schooling to learning.

A new vampire of unknown, traces Victor and he wants to take revenge for all defeats. Victor will be under tremendous stress, his combat and outcome will alter his future. Does he conquer or gives up – follows in next chapter.

Chapter – 11

"The Finest Cut and Moving on"

The Vampire of Unknown

Imagine, when someone makes you unconscious, and cuts you apart. The feel to get our body parts cut makes us shudder with fear, since four years, Victor has been working for the same company. He has a proven track record of excellence, quality and results. He is now level two in the hierarchy after Robin Steve.

Robin too leaves responsibilities on his competent shoulders and focuses on expansion, the time is good for the company, customers and employees. Victor now gets a handsome pay package and is pleased with his life. He helps needy people.

He learns new specialisms and uses them in practical circumstances. He diligently follows the application of knowledge as a routine habit.

He believes, Knowledge without application is like a cloth which you will never wear. Either discard it or use it, otherwise, it will consume the space which we can utilize for other purposes.

Lots of graduate from prestigious business schools had joined Victor in the past years, and he could easily catch the gap which keeps them mediocre. Sometimes he wonders why these institutions charge so heavily, when they do not contribute pragmatic cognizance and spot-on values in their students.

Through his experiences, he has understood the power of helping people in their early careers, and he succors those pass outs to kill their unique vampires. He believes that trust is the foundation of any relationship, he works to create an environment of credibility and care where people can focus on the quality of work rather balance power equations with top management. He cancels the superfluous meetings, where the underlying agenda is to show managers busy. Instead, he changes those to fewer open sessions to bring more productive outcomes. Open management becomes a culture of his organization, people can informally walk in and discuss their issues.

Many fictitious activities were presented to management to show value additions of teams, the slides work. Victor is against any hypocritical approach toward life and work so he takes it with Robin, and they determine to call a spade a spade.

They work jointly to create a company culture which is productive and yet free from fear. It becomes a VOW organization to work for.

Victor had learned the concept of fear in the past, now he had become the force which has taken the fear away from the entire organization. People feel more confident now, they take ownership, actions are much faster and efficient and instead to spend the time to show themselves busy, they ask for real additional responsibilities to fill their spare capacity.

His contagious attitude has spread across the organization, and he often gets lucrative offers from industry to join them. With all best efforts, he establishes himself as a tremendously successful brand. People love him and like to work with him, he is their true leader. Not only he is a people's leader, but also he exceeds the company goals in terms of profitability. The company skyrockets, and Victor continues to make masterful application of his knowledge.

To succeed in life, you need to apply what you have learned.

"Knowledge will not attract money, unless it is organized, and intelligently directed, through practical Plans of Action, to the Definite End of accumulation of money. Lack of understanding of this fact has been the source of confusion to millions of people who falsely believe that "knowledge is power." It is nothing of the sort! Knowledge is only potential power. It becomes power only when, and if, it is organized into definite

plans of action, and directed to a definite end." –
Napoleon Hill

Success follows efforts if efforts are genuine, and you keep a check and consistently rectify errors, you are sure to thrive. Always ruminate about what can be done better, what could be done differently. He publishes fundamentals which help people succeed:

Set Goals

"You are never too old to set another goal or to dream a new dream." - C. S. Lewis

Bigger success needs - multiplication of actions, the addition of knowledge, a division of goals (short term and long term), subtraction of excuses and the correct values.

He sets goals and reviews them regularly. He completes professional courses through distance education, it makes him more desirable for management roles. One, who desires to climb higher in life, must prepare himself well. Unless you have goals written on paper, you tend to forget it quickly. People who write goals, have a clear direction, they guard and keep their eyes on the goals, and do not to allow any interference on the way to achieve those goals. Also, he makes it a practice of the people he had met. He has developed so much faith in these ideas that he magnifies those to the utmost levels. He does better than his mentors and trains hundreds of people. He sets another goal for a bigger benefit- the benefit of a community "Enable, Multiply, Succeed". He had learned to apply the art of multiplication, the simple multiplication taught in the schools, higher the multiplier higher the yields.

If you can think and write, you need to put it on a piece of paper and regularly review it. This list inspires you to take actions.

Dress Right

"Being well dressed is a beautiful form of politeness."

-Donna Bobana

He dresses well and believes people who do not care about themselves cannot take care of others. As per him not to dress well is a sign of non-commitment.

There is a high need that people dress to impress. We feel fantastic to meet a decent and well-groomed person, the same applies to them as well. If we need others also to feel good in meeting us, we need to follow the same. It's our responsibility that the dignity of the workplace uplifts not downgrades by our dressing sense. His team also follows the same. Whenever there is a meeting, his team stands out. Not only are they impressive intrinsically but also extrinsically. This spells a magical mantra on customers, and the company counts cash through substantial add-on businesses. It's a merry time for all.

When you dress well, you attract more people. Specifically in a workplace, you feel a difference when your seniors notice you and take you more seriously. If you are young you appear mature and more cultured which is beneficial. If you are old, you look elegant and more youthful.

When people notice your seriousness about appearances, they feel that you will do alike in all other fields of your life. They get the assurance that their work is in the right hands. Dress to attract success.

Keep One hour for Self

"Learn to work harder on yourself than you do on your job. If you work hard on your job you'll make a living, if you work hard on yourself you can make a fortune." –
Jim Rohn

He brings training culture back to the company. No, he does not re-establish the "Training Department" dissolved three years back. Being aware that cost pressure is a necessary evil, he starts training employees after office hours and he does it willingly compared to what his senior did under pressure – Same things done with different attitude and approach create different impacts. He calls this, "One Hour For Self." This program becomes so successful that a lot of good managers grow out of it and those always surplus the skilled workforce requirement.

He tells people "Just 1 hour, please keep it for yourself, and see the difference."

You can understand this by a very simple example; if you put one hour on your health or to learn and meditate the benefits which follow are evident. Begin with one day, you feel different, and that difference holds you to continue. If you do not feel the difference, please do not hold to it, do something which suits you, but make some progress. Rather than to wait for good events in your life, you need to learn, apply and make them happen. Do not wait for the rain, dig a canal to irrigate your farms. If you wait for rain, and it does not rain, you will face the drought.

Slowly people notice an aura build around you, they do not catch the difference because that remains your secret. If they come to you and ask, please share with them. Generously distribute knowledge to the seekers.

Good Leadership

"If your actions inspire others to dream more, learn more, do more and become more, you are a leader."

-John Quincy Adams

You are a leader when, you read, you learn, you walk the talk, you listen, you deliver, you honor, and you make others successful. That's how you become a leader.

Do you ever brood over, why so many books are written on leadership and management? The books which sell in millions are always written on the topics of significance. More than that, everyone has a strong desire to lead, why? Because leaders make a difference, they impact the lives to make it better. Right skillset is a must to turn you into a good leader, if you notice the effects of World Wars on humanity that is what a bad leadership consequences. The world survives on the shoulders of good leaders. There is a need to bring inner leader out and multiply the impact. No one stops you to lead, if you lead yourself, if you lead among friends, if you lead in school, if you lead at home or work, you are a leader. When you lead, you are in charge of your life and you command your life, you know which direction you need to go and succeed.

Victor studies the biographies of successful individuals, surf business news and reads self-help books. He develops new interests and meets his goals. Wise leaders are readers and readers are leaders, they do read minimum one worthwhile paragraph a day.

Fitness Promise

"Physical fitness is not only one of the most important keys to a healthy body, it is the basis of dynamic and creative intellectual activity." John F. Kennedy

Fitness keeps you in the best form and free from ailments. This is a virtue which keeps you motivated, to succeed your energy levels must be high, and regular exercise helps achieve that. One step at a time if not more, start with ten minutes a day. Do not run, do not lift weights at the go, initiate with breath control. Deep conscious breathing. Be aware of the breath, inhale, halt and exhale, you do not essentially need a track, sports shoes or gymnasium– your body, time and the floor are more than sufficient.

As Sylvester Stallone shared, 'I'm not a genetically superior person. I built my body'. This gift God has blessed you with, and you must respect that.

When Victor starts, he undergoes additional pain to lift weights, makes the extra effort. He finds that exercise is more about psychological and physical fitness, it prepares you to lift more and bear the pain. Makes you more tolerant, and you do not mind to run the last mile or an added mile, do a few reps heavier. The best point to learn from exercise is 'consistency', you need to do it daily to sustain the effects. It helps him to understand, no results are permanent without consistent efforts. It's 'Kaizen', a continuous improvement process.

Back to the situation 'The Vampire of the unknown' is ready to strike upon Victor and his family.

Victor receives a phone call in office, he gets in dismay and shock, his mother had a stroke, and he has been told that though the doctors have managed to save her life, she needs to undergo a bypass surgery to avoid life risk. The hospitals in his hometown had no medical facilities to operate. Her condition is not good, and his brother brings her to the capital city. Victor had already lost his father, and he does not want to lose his mother. To lose our people is the worst feel which one can ever have. He is now capable and financially successful. Next day Prince, brings her to the city hospital in a state of unconsciousness. Victor rushes to the hospital, it is a large hospital overcrowded with patients. Victor knows that to get an appointment here will be a task, he also notices the poor patients have no options than to wait, poverty is a curse and millions lose their lives waiting for treatments. Victor had never visited any hospital earlier.

Victor knows what to do at this moment, he thinks quickly and has money and resources. His mind races as he wants to save his mother's life at any cost. There are other well-known hospitals in the city which charged high. He takes an immediate decision to shift her to another hospital. The doctor in the hospital is an excellent cardiologist, and he immediately understands the criticality of the situation. They move her to the ICU (Intensive Care Unit). The doctors, nurses, ward boys and technicians rush to the place and make all efforts to save her.

Victor makes a payment over the counter. Money is helpful in all cases if used correctly. Besides pay your bills it helps to save lives, educate kids, help others and keeps you confident. You must earn good money to avoid any guilt in future that you would have done any differently if you had it. Victor recalls that, he used to discuss in his group that money is nothing, it's only the love and care which matters. Love and care are the most precious assets in life. The problem with the statement "Money is not important" is that it serves as a weak excuse for the failures to earn. People put the blame of financial failures on love and care to justify that they concentrate more on love and care and hence do not focus on money. There is no logic behind it, to earn money does not stop you from loving and caring more, the smart efforts make all of them bond and grow mutually, and if one increases, the others do not necessarily decrease. Increase all of them, use them mutually to grow more. Make money by the work you love and spend on the people you love, take advantage of it to take care of needy people. All these are interrelated and can grow together. Today, Victor is able to save his loving mother with the help of money.

"The lack of money is the root of all evil."

- Mark Twain

With his hardships Victor had learned the importance of money, this incident makes him realize it's worth much more. He opens his notebook and reads 'commitment to yourself': That always - I will value time, money, people, and nation.

The hospital conducts all required tests to check if his mother is ready to operate. She is not in a good state, the operation can be very risky. The doctor instructs his team to shift her to life-saving equipment. He had handled many complex cases in the past and wanted to go ahead with the operation. He calls Victor and his brother, Prince to take consent and informs them of the situation, there is no other option. He also advises that emergency six units of blood will be required, which they need to arrange. The blood bank had a shortage as it was a rare blood group. Victor calls Robin Steve to update on the situation and requests him to announce the need for blood donation. The idea works, they get ample of donators, and Robin rushes all of them to the hospital. He yet again proves why he is so successful in his life. He takes a genuine interest in the life of people. The employees who come for blood donations are among the people he had trained and they truly regard him. They empathize, "Your mother is our mother Victor, and we will do anything for her." Victor's eyes fill with tears, he had never imagined that his efforts would pay back in this manner. It is not only the money but also the love and care which join their hands to save his mother's life. In advance of the operation, Doctor stops near Victor and assures,

"Rest assured, it will be **The Finest Cut** I have ever done, and everything will be all right."

His mother goes to the operation theater, unconscious, and the doctors are ready to operate on her, and this is when he realizes that even under such critical circumstances people trust and are hopeful to get well, as it saves their lives. He notices that the reason for this trust is the skill of the person, the doctor is also a normal human, who acquires the skills through education and practice. He also trains on the right equipment and experience to handle life.

After a couple of hours, the Doctor came out of the Operation Theater and rejoiced, "Congratulations, the operation is successful, she is conscious and has shown outstanding signs of recovery. You can go and meet her after an hour."

Victor and his brother hug each other and Doctor joins them. Victor is able to save his mother. The vampire of Unknown got killed by the Angels of Love, care and money. After a couple of days, hospital discharges her. She decides to stay with Victor for rest of her life as the city has best medical facilities. He had always wanted his mother to stay with him ever since he started earning well, his dream finally came true.

Now, Victor is back to routine life, he thinks about the difference in the two hospitals. One would have magnified his mother's critical condition, the other has saved her life. He remembers the term Doctor had used "The Finest Cut." As the seeds of this concept have sprouted during his hospital experience, he names it

"The Finest Cut Concept"

"We've all got both light and dark inside us. What matters is the part we choose to act on. That's who we really are." – J.K. Rowling

He compares his experience of both hospitals, skills and expertise were constant factors. He knows that knowledge, skills and experience are the founding stones and notices below for differences

1. Delay vs. Urgency

2. Haze vs. Fact

3. Hostility vs. Hospitality

4. Incredulity vs. Assurance

Victor further looks into all scenarios in life. How would you like to be treated, and how would you treat others?

Victor takes the qualities from the good hospital and develops them into 'The Finest Cut Concept'.

Sense of urgency:

When they had reached the second hospital, staff showed a commendable sense of urgency to deal with the situation, whereas the first hospital had lengthy queues. This can relate to the situations when you get some work, and you have a long list of priorities with you. Every case links with life and death, delays end up as a dead goal, project, business or idea. The biggest killer of all serial killers is procrastination.

The sense of urgency does not translate to the centralization of actions, then it becomes micromanagement and poor delegation. It only means that once a case comes, you need to take urgent action and connect it to the able people. This time is not to show your authority or importance. There are millions of instances where a person mismanages to send information, reasons can be many – travel, vacation, meetings or simply an oversight. On last day, it comes to the team as a most urgent task which must finish here and now. Make plans, delegate it to the right people. If you are away, send an auto message to give contact details for your back-up. If you do not have a backup, you lack abilities as a person and a manager. It's as a person dies in a road accident and his spouse does not have the details of his accounts, insurance policies, and emergency contact numbers. All information to handle urgencies must be in easy reach.

Haze vs. Truth:

The truth is not bitter it's the tone you use to present it, that makes mind perceive it in a negative connotation.

When they reached the other hospital, they had a clear view of the process, blood requirement, critical health information and whereas at the first hospital, they had no visibility even on getting an appointment. The second hospital shared all requirements, backed with plans, full visibility of the actions to be taken, the risks involved and the recommended course of action as per the need of the hour. Facts represent honesty in your approach. Whenever someone comes to you, tell facts and propose best options, it helps them to decide on the right option. In case there are no choices, proceed with the only choice and inform them. As Buddha preached -"Three things cannot be long hidden: the sun, the moon, and the truth."

There is no need to hide. Candor is the foundation of credibility, people take the time to understand you but once the results turn out dead-on they respect your truthfulness.

The truth is not bitter it's the tone you use to tell it.

Hostility vs. Hospitality:

In the second hospital, the staff had touched their hearts with generosity, they took good care whereas in the first hospital, no one appeared concerned. A good hospitality can do wonders, you retain your customers, and they recommend you to others at zero advertisement cost. When you grow giant, your attitude becomes indirectly-hostile. You build several vain processes to make yourself unapproachable. Be generous, remove the barriers and create an open, hospitable environment. You need to be cordial to strangers, guests and all alike.

Today the world lives a life of experiences, good hospitality is the best experience you can give.

Incredulity vs. Assurance:

The first hospital had created an environment which made it difficult to believe them. The second hospital had created an environment of assurance through their actions and words. We need not give only verbal assurance all times. Most of the times it is the body language which provides assurance, he remembers the moment when the doctor had joined the hug. Whenever we deal with a person or an organization, our body language and actions must be in sync. These must affirm their choice is correct to hand over the business to you. You can craft an affirmation which suits their conditions perfectly, it makes them believe that the goals would be met. Remember that real actions support your assurance. Assurance does not equal results, it is the first step of commitment to yourself that you promise none less than your best. Right assurance is the cement to build trust if right actions support it.

Some experts produce impressive work, however when they forget to add their Finest Cut into it, it brings down the quality to below average. It's like to build the most magnificent structure of the world and keep it undecorated and unfinished, people see how enormous it is or how much money you spend on the building. But as it remains as an unfinished, undecorated task no one appreciates it.

No one likes to buy an apartment where the builder has a bad reputation not to complete the projects. Their future projects are hard to sell, the firm enter o loss and heads toward bankruptcy. It's your life, to make it momentous add The Finest Cut in everything you do.

Once you do it, it becomes a trait of your personality, and you need not practice it anymore. However, a refresher on regular intervals is recommended.

The difference between what we do and what we are capable of doing would suffice to solve most of the world's problems. 		- Mahatma Gandhi

Victor integrates this into his personality and gets fabulous results. He establishes his name beyond the borders too, and now organizations from different countries want to hire him, it is time to move on, he already has everything he wanted from life. This country had amply rewarded him for his deeds, he had good terms with Robin Steve, highly trusted by his team and respected in Industry. Why would he move?

Chapter – 12

"Emotions and Spread your Goodness."

Concept and Meeting with Patrick

The Vampire of Limitation

A wealthy landowner cannot cultivate and improve his farm without spreading comfort and well-being around him. Rich and abundant crops, a numerous population and a prosperous countryside are the rewards for his efforts.   *-Antoine Lavoisier*

Victor often receives calls from global companies who want to hire him but he feels deeply connected to his current organization. He acutely regarded his team members and business partners, the government has recently awarded him with community welfare award for his new skills development program for the youth. He has it all, homes, cars, and a solid bank balance. He discreetly helps the underprivileged, for this purpose, he has done a survey. Initially, he wanted to support kids who wished to study further but could not afford the fees. Survey gave a totally different prospect, he had found parents took excellent care of their kids and they make all possible efforts to give them a good life. In fact, in most of the families people ignored old parents who had no income or savings. Also, widows have difficulties raising their kids. He had started to help such people, there are many aged parents and widows who had benefitted due to his efforts. He was here not only to take from the society but also to give back.

He is happy and contented with his life. There are no gripping reasons to make a move and leave his home country. His emotions get on the way to make a decision. Money always remains important but it does not drive him anymore, he already has enough passive income sources through the investments he has done.

He decides to meet Patrick and seek his advice on the matter. Apart from other reasons, he also needs clarification on commitment to yourself:

> Always I will value time, money, people and nation.

Is it not, that if he leaves his mother nation, he will go against his commitment which he has followed so religiously? He wants to discuss this with Patrick before he takes the final call. Although he was not able to meet Patrick often, but he stayed connected on special occasions such as birthday, New Year and festivals. He calls and fixes an appointment.

"Your mentors are your best treasures, always make conscious efforts to stay in touch, they are the reason behind your success."

After a gap of five years they meet again, both are very happy and excited.

Patrick, "Hey Vick, so good to see you in person. You have made it big and that too in a short span of time. Let me make a cup of coffee and we will talk about it. I want to know every bit of detail."

Victor senses the glee in Patrick's voice, he smiles and reciprocates, "All because of you, my angel, all the credit goes to you."

"I Love your modesty Vick, I have helped dozens of people in a similar way, even when I have made more efforts they gave up very easily. You have done the best ever, and you are in the news too. You have truly lived the concepts." He hands over the coffee mug to Victor,

"So my friend, can you show it to me how to do that? I am superbly, truly, exceptionally delighted with your stupendous success."

"Sure Pat, I am equally excited to update my progress to you. After I had got the job, I made consistent efforts and lived up to the concepts I had learned from you – so far I have been able to kill all vampires which had targeted to turn me into a slave. Every day, without fail I have refreshed my concepts and I always keep my notebook with me. See, it's with me right now as well."

Patrick notices it is the same notebook, he had seen the first time Victor shared his notes with him.

"I lived by the concept of Integrity within yourself, overcame the vampires of fear, always followed the Commitment to yourself, and multiplied the 'Eight scenarios of internal happiness'. I went one step further and spread it across the community through multiplication methods, each one teaches one. I developed the concept of Desired Personality, I had learned the concept of Decision-Making the Right Way from Robin Steve. As you rightly told, I have learned it on the job under practical scenarios. I learned to Communicate for Opportunities, and my mother's operation led me to the discovery of The Finest Cut concept. I applied and multiplied all these concepts at various forums. As committed to you and Colonel Michael Barr, I have passed acquired knowledge and experience to all who come across. I have developed the concept to Multiply Your Luck as well".

Patrick "Wow you sure figured it out fast, the way you have summarized the concepts exhibit that you truthfully live up to these values. Because of your sincerity, you were able to bring people together to achieve bigger objectives and uplifted the whole society." Patrick attentively listens to Victor, he takes a sip from his coffee mug and further asks,

"A few things you have developed are new, you have shared The Finest Cut and Communicate for opportunities in our phone calls. But 'Multiply you Luck' is entirely new for me. I am interested to know, can people multiply their luck as well?"

Victor smiles and looks at Patrick, "Sure Pat, am happy to share that, but preceding to that, I have a question which I will like to ask you."

Patrick allowed "Sure."

"Pat you were successful when I met you, it was you who held my hand and made me walk on the right track. I honestly give the credit of my success to you, the concepts which have made hundreds of people successful originated from you."

Victor stops for a moment, Patrick is beholding at him, guessing the question which was on the way. Victor continues,

"When I met you for the first time, I had this question in my mind, and I have held it for so long. Now I want to ask this – Why do you live in this place when you are so successful and wealthy, you can easily afford the nicest place in the city, wherever you want?"

Patrick laughs, "You have not missed a thing, and no need to hold such questions for long Vick."

There are two reasons behind it, one I do live by the principle that rich people must live below their means. Secondly, the purpose of my life is the welfare of the community, especially underprivileged. Here, I find more people who need my guidance and can become a success story like you. Tell me Vick, would you have found me if I had lived in a posh expanse, confined by access control systems and security guards?

When I became successful, the needs of these people turned me toward philanthropy, like it had touched Mother Teresa in the past. I wish to remain accessible to all needy people for the whole of my life. This is the philosophy which I live by. Even if I move to a different location I will stay in such ambiance. Rather than spend my money and time on luxuries I prefer to bequeath."

"Help others and give something back. I guarantee you will discover that while public service improves the lives and the world around you, its greatest reward is the enrichment and new meaning it will bring to your own life." - Arnold Schwarzenegger

Patrick had monumental faith in his philosophy. In our society, there are only a few like him, who regard those people who looked for help. Patrick shared that he did not restrict at thoughts, he took massive actions to make it real. He has helped people by clarifying their concepts. He also had set-up a nonprofit organization in the neighborhood, where people get free consultations and learn the best practices for life.

Victor understands, "Pat, you are a spiritual incarnation and now onwards I will call you Guru. I entirely agree that if you had not met me five years ago, my life would have been completely different."

He gets back to Patrick's question, "During this time, I read books by world-class authors and watched their videos as well. One of the stories touched me greatly, and I would like to share it with you.

There was a young man, Emanuel James, raised in the land of obscurity he could not do well, he was directionless and surrounded by all sort of problems and challenges. Creditors were chasing him for payments, he had no money to support his living. One of his friends took him to a seminar, influenced by the lecture he resigned from the job and joined to work under this entrepreneur. His mentor asked him about his list of goals, he had no list. Mentor observed, "If you do not have a list of goals your bank balance had to be less than a few hundred dollars." So he set his list of goals, kept checking them and it worked. His life changed significantly, later he built one of the largest organizations. From a farmland boy, Emanuel James became a millionaire. He developed a unique and simple philosophy on personal development which turned the life of millions. Though in the initial six years he struggled with life, in the next five to six years he became a millionaire" Victor stops for a moment. "This shows how significant can be the impacts of the right mentorship. Pat, you are my guru and whenever I read this story, it reminded me of you. There has never been a day when I have not followed the concepts you taught me, I practiced and lived up to those values.' He further continues the story,

"He developed more concepts, and trained millions of people, still the world knows him by the name of late great Jim Rohn, The Millionaire Maker, and his mentor was late John Earl Shoaff the entrepreneur, and he was President and Board Chairman of the Nutri-Bio Corporation. I wish I could have met them in person."

Patrick hears the story, his eyes get wet as Victor's high veneration for him touches his heart. He too has easily forgotten like all others who went ahead in life and never looked back. Though he had never expected anyone to say thanks for his mentorship, still he has felt awesome to see his efforts producing results. It confirmed that the path of vision and mission he has undertaken heads in the right direction. Victor is proved most successful among the persons he had shared his knowledge with, no one had achieved heights like him.

He is a brilliant mentor soul with classic behavior and virtue.

The dream had begun with his faith, he had pushed Victor to the next level and created an exemplary shift in his thoughts.

He rejoices, "Thanks Vick, for all the trust and the respect you have for me. I feel proud that you have kept your learnings on and spread the legacy of goodness on a large scale. I will like to hear about the 'Multiply your Luck' concept, which is new to me. Perhaps I will be able to apply the same and increase my service to the community."

Multiply your luck

"You gotta try your luck at least once a day, because you could be going around lucky all day and not even know it."- Jimmy Dean

Victor explains, "Sure. I had learned the "Eight Internal Happiness Scenarios" from you, which opened me to the principle of multiplication. I intentionally concentrated on the extents where it can be applied. Robin Steve used to travel a lot. Being number two, I represented the organization on various forums. I did that well and achieved good growth, but I did not call it a noteworthy success. Sometimes I noticed that my presence was not enough to convince customers and win more business, and we were not the preferred choice. I relentlessly meditated about it, why we failed and finally, I arrived at a conclusion that even if it is luck, what can be done to make it better. That brought me to the concept of Multiply Your Luck.

I conducted detailed research on the companies and their culture, I studied all the deals we had lost to our competition. It was not the cost or plans that failed us. I worked hard to figure out the difference which made competition win the deals.

I followed all the concepts I had learned so far, I opened my notebook and read a commitment,

I will make a difference and make consistent efforts

It sparked a whole new thinking process, I noticed that during the years I had focused on productivity, and that was yielding magnificent results. There was still something amiss, and I was trying to figure it out. While we were at the peak level of productivity, the level of creativity was low. With all best efforts, we were able to retain business and add some more. However there is a difference between good and great, the champions win or lose merely by the fraction of a second. The commitment of making a difference encircled my brain, I analyzed that we did our business in a standard yet outdated way, we followed the same hierarchal approach as all others. Why there should be a difference in results if everyone follows the same?

On a midnight, I called Robin and told him that I wanted to discuss something urgent and after one hour we were at a coffee shop.

Robin heard the idea, he was not sure about it but he asked to proceed as his faith on me was over his preference to methodical approach.

He told me, "We can only increase our chances to win by this, there is no negative impact to try it, go ahead, spread your wings and fly, think innovative and make sure there are no additional costs."

I found that a particular pattern existed in won and lost deals. I started following that pattern, till this time I had not discussed it with anyone apart from Robin. I wanted to confirm whether my actions were in the right direction. We crafted and organized new flexible team structures. Those teams used to meet specific customers in my and Robin's absence, even when we both were available, we skipped the meetings. The effects were astonishingly positive for the organization. Our business started to multiply. From being unlucky, we started being the luckiest and our competitors were startled. Today this concept is known as 'Multiply Your Luck' in the organization, and this is a secret strategy for our exceptional success.

You would be surprised what people can deliver, and not exceptional people, normal people can produce miraculous outcomes. When the right person reaches the right place, you can get all the results you want."

Victor stops as he sips coffee,

"When I researched, I found that competition has same hierarchal systems in their companies. However we had more young salesmen in our organization as compared to the competition and that was due to the cost saving strategy. I noticed that most of the deals we won were from new startups, whereas competitors won the other deals. We further found that our competitors were winning the deals where customers expected more matured people to present the business proposals to them. Also, there were companies that looked for women leadership in the teams, and the startups wanted to see the youth submit the plans to them. There was a need to bring more equality regarding gender and age within our team."

Patrick intervened, "So you directed company's focus on creativity and quality toward hiring employees based on gender equality and age group."

"No Pat, I did not do that, cost effectiveness is the core of our organizational strategy, and our customers love us for that, they need the best quality at lowest price. That would have been an easy solution, and anybody could have guessed about that. We did differently.

Previous to this idea, I was in the dark on how to proceed, I had no clarity on what could be done, and perhaps that made me feel like an owl. This condition reminded me of a past incident when I had seen an owl at home, I wanted to hit it with a stone and make it fly. My mother stopped me from doing that. When I asked for the reason, she told me an interesting story, "It is the owl of Minerva — my dad had told me that it is the favorite bird of Goddess Athena, the goddess of wisdom, war and the crafts. The bird is a symbol of knowledge, intelligence and sophistication. Even Hindu mythology tells that this bird belongs to the Goddess of wealth, Lakshmi. If you hurt him, the Goddess might get upset with you."

I started thinking about the bird. I wondered why the goddesses would keep a bird which humans refer to a dumb person. But my brain alarmed, "Hey! Wake up, this is exactly opposite of what the bird is supposed to be."

Owl is the only bird which can see in the dark. It can turn its neck three sixty degrees which no other creature can do, though scientific studies suggest that it can only turn up to two seventy degrees, I still went with the assumption of three sixty degrees as that mythical fact was more helpful for me to find a solution.

I connected owl's ability to see in the dark to the vision which can see the opportunities others cannot see. The neck rotation of three sixty degrees, resembled with the exploration of all options around you. The owl's virtue made me move out of my cabin to the floor, to see in the dark with the three sixty degrees angle. I scanned people in my organization, we had both, a combination of matured and young male and female employees, which was sufficient to implement my idea to win business. The issue was, they had no hands-on experience to meet customers and work on the proposals. We cross trained the resources and unswervingly worked on training the new members, developed their skills, did the job rotations and took massive actions. After six months, we had what we wanted at zero additional cost.

The combination team we created to work on customer proposals, created more leaders from both genders. This entirely changed the game, customers were happy with the care taken to deal with their requirements, the team was happy with their development and the organization with growth in its revenue. Engagement levels increased and that significantly reflected on our business line. The company was at the top in a few months which meant more opportunities and better raises for all.

Everyone can be better than yesterday, I was able to kill the vampire of limitation that made us stick to the hierarchical approach. People followed this religiously and the experience they gained by doing this helped in a glorious fashion, it multiplied everybody's luck.

So my opportunity of being lucky multiplied several times by using the luck of others. They were luckier than me in many deals, they were miraculous, and the company never looked back after that. The team earned various rewards for processes innovation, cost reduction, and improved gender biased inequality." Victor pauses and waits for Patrick's remarks.

"Trust is a core currency of any relationship. Sometimes our need to control and micromanage everything erodes our confidence in ourselves and others. The truth: People are much more capable than we think. A hearty dose of trust is often what's needed to unlock the magic. Go ahead, have faith." - Kris Carr

Patrick: "Wow that's marvelous, you chiseled a solution with the combination of commitment to yourself, from your childhood experience and created trust in people. Not only Robin but also entire team demonstrated a strong faith in your concept, which happens only when people truly trust you.

I need to figure it out that how I can imbibe this into my learnings. As a first go, I can replicate it in my organization. Also, I need to explore how it will help the needy.

Initially, it might appear different, but any new idea needs a change in existing thinking which people find hard to accept and adapt. You have already proven its sequels and if others applied it, it is sure to work.

I do remember a few instances, when I had sent someone else to complete the projects, and they did exceptionally well. Perhaps I forget to consider the fact how lucky they were for me, and I could have multiplied it in the future. We need to keep our wisdom handy, see three sixty degrees in the dark and advance best person to handle the job."

Victor takes the last sip of coffee and echoes,

"Yes, we have luck spread around us in abundance, we need to feel it and figure out a way to multiply it."

Patrick, "Yes I agree, so next is what? You wanted to discuss the new opportunities you are getting from overseas.

Is there something I can help with?"

Victor: "Yes Pat, you are the greatest help I ever had in my life, I want to discuss it with you. Now that I receive multiple calls from organizations to join them, it makes me think whether it would be a right decision to move out or not. Though I am quick at decision making, I am not able to conclude on this. My country has given me everything, Robin Steve treats me as a brother, and I feel that it would be unfair to leave.

I want your opinion on this, what would be the right course of action?

Always I will value time, money, people and nation.

Isn't it against this commitment to my people and nation? This feeling intrudes and confuddles me."

Patrick replies, "Vick, I deliberated on this as you had shared with me on call, I have taken help from Colonel Michael Barr and a few other notable people to arrive at a conclusion. Honestly, it was a tough stranger question for me too."

Victor, "Ah you met Colonel Barr, I wish I could have been there with you to see him. Is he fine?"

Patrick: "Yes, he is vigorous than ever, always full of courage and life, he has read your news and told me to pass on his blessings to you. He is proud of your accomplishments."

Victor: "I am honored, if I will decide to leave this country I would definitely pay a visit to him before I depart. But what conclusion did you come to?"

Patrick pauses for a moment, takes a deep breath and the wisdom of a sage came out, "We concluded that………

You must accept the opportunities and move on."

Victor had not expected this to be the final decision, he was not inclined to leave his people and country, and he was hopeful that if he gets support on his preference, he will discard all proposals that come to him. He asks,

"I am interested to know the aspects to arrive at this decision."

Patrick, "Yes, it's a natural question."

They move up to the roof of the building, it was open there, Patrick continues,

"What is bothering you is the commitment to yourself, once your doubts are clear, you will feel comfortable with this decision. Also, note that this is our opinion and the final decision is still yours, I am sharing what we perceive is appropriate."

Like always Victor carefully listens to Patrick,

"Always I will value time, money, people and nation- we will not discuss time and money here as you will have the same hours, more money and efficient ways to utilize your strengths. The question in your mind is related to people and nation.

First of all, I will again remind you of phrase in Hindu Maha-Upanishad "Vasudhaiva Kutumbakam" which means "The World is One Family."

If you truly value people, you should not differentiate them by nationality, gender, race, color, region or religion. All are members of your family, you have Robin Steve here, you would find Zhou Chan in Asia, and Malcolm Harris in Europe. The people will come and go, each will touch your life in a different manner.

You have rapidly risen above the ranks, and earned so much goodness to share, you must spread it to as many people as you could. Actually, you should make multiple efforts to increase the circle of goodness.

What if the companies who discover latest technologies, education and systems do not share it with other countries? An invention is done in one country, manufactured in other and sold in a third country, this is how it becomes a source of global success.

What if the air we breathe, says, I belong to only one country and will not flow in others? There would be deaths across.

What if the Sun says, I will pass my rays only to one region and not others? There would be total darkness.

What if clouds, oceans and rivers say, we belong only to one location? There would be droughts all around.

What if parents say, I will love only one kid and not others?

There are no favorites when these natural powers decide to distribute their goodness. We are also a piece of nature, why should we restrict?

I know you are not afraid of solitude, I know you will do great, and you will think infinite. Apart from that, I have strong faith that the goodness which you will spread across the globe would change the life of millions in future."

Patrick stops and questions Vick: "Are you now comfortable to accept the opportunity and live up to the philosophy of Vasudhaiva Kutumbakam?"

Victor thinks deeply, his brain is open to consume the thoughts which Patrick has passed to him, and it is the advice of wise people who had achieved significantly in life. He has answered his question related to people. However he still finds the justification weak to leave his country and asks:

"What about my country Patrick, I am born and brought up here, mother nation has provided everything I need.

I like the idea of spread goodness across the world, also, I accept not to differentiate people by nationality, gender, race, color, region or religion. But why I cannot stay in my country and do that, why I need to move out? Cannot I stay here and help the people around, like you."

Patrick with a deep sense of compassion looks at Victor and responds,

"When we move out of our nation, we represent our country to the world, if we are great, they honor us with the highest national awards. Thus, we make our nation stronger globally, and the goodness of our country spreads across. People feel brilliant about our country and people.

Though we have people from many countries who won pride for their motherland, I would like to quote Indians here, the country has its own challenges, power failures, pollution, water scarcity, poor infrastructure, slow decision-making, poverty, and corruption. But it still has the talent which enabled its people to lead world's biggest organizations and pour goodness.

Fellow Indians feel proud of them as they spread hope and courage in them that they too can grow. Indra Nooyi PepsiCo, Vikram Pandit Citibank, Sundar Pichai Google Inc. and Satya Nadella, Microsoft are the examples of Indian origin Americans, and we have all heard about their stories. They have made it to the list of most influential people. If the people from the countries with such difficult circumstances can rise and spread the goodness across the globe, what stops us from doing that?

And if you talk about me, why you cannot stay here like me. I need to accept that I have not multiplied the concepts to the magnitude you did, I have learned the concepts from others and followed those. I have also not developed any concepts on my own, your concepts are original, and you will create few more with time.

Vick, you have impacted and revolutionized my belief. If I can bring myself up to the level of your understanding and application, I too would like to spread the opportunities across boundaries. You are ready, I am not. You cannot go beyond the level of practical application of your thoughts.

You have mixed and multiplied various success concepts and made sure that those are implemented to produce best outcomes.

Now earn pride for your country, this would be the multiplication of commitment toward valuing your country. We have unparalleled hopes on you, now it is the time to spread that hope across."

Do not let the 'Vampire of Limitation' bite you.

Victor's brain become enthused by the vibes Patrick passed to him. The output is equivalent to input, after going through a process. He was not needy but feel to win pride for the country on a larger forum, helps overcome the limitations, and spreading goodness to all excites him.

Chapter – 13

"Feelings, Emotions and Decisions"

The Vampire of wrong tool selection

"Take up one idea. Make that one idea your life - think of it, dream of it, live on that idea. Let the brain, muscles, nerves, every part of your body, be full of that idea, and just leave every other idea alone. This is the way to success". -

Swami Vivekananda

Victor spends that night at Patrick's home and goes back to his office in the morning. He has decided to move on, the world waits for him, he desires to win pride for his nation and spread the concepts to the people of the world.

However, he still has to discuss it with Robin, he wants to leave their strong relationship on a positive note. Robin is on a trip so he sends him an email, he mentions his desire to quit the job.

Sometimes it's helpful to convey your feelings in writing, when you write your thoughts, you can review, rewrite and make required corrections. Writing presents thoughts in an organized manner. Always practice writing when you feel that in discussions, you might get drifted away by a counter thought or question.

He feels good after he sends the message, which signals that the decision is right. Though Robin is on a holiday trip, he reads and hurls back the email.

"I am coming back, we will discuss and decide. I would be there tomorrow, let us meet out of office in the evening."

Victor spends rest of his day to review the actions of his team, he takes them out for lunch.

At lunch, he thinks that he would miss all who have worked so closely toward joint goals and made him immensely efficacious. He can never pay for the support they have given. He was very attached to them.

He does not share anything with the team as he was waiting to meet Robin. This matter was a highly confidential, once Robin agrees, management will communicate it to the team.

Next evening Robin Steve comes back to the town, they meet on the roof-top of a five-star hotel. Robin is serious as the discussion is of significant importance to him. Victor had a unique respect for Robin, he feels calm inside. Robin orders a glass of wine and a mocktail for Victor, and starts the conversation.

"Victor, what has happened suddenly, why do you want to leave the organization, I have left entire responsibilities on you, and you are getting what you want, do you need more?

It has come to me as a sudden surprise, I never thought that you would think in this direction. Let me know what you want?"

Victor concurs, "Robin, I can understand how you feel, I have very high regards for you. You are not only my boss, but also elder brother and mentor too. You are an icon for me, and you have inspired me throughout. I love the company and the country. This time is emotional for me, but I believe that the purpose of my life is to spread the concepts to all, beyond geographical reach and any political boundaries. I have loved your leadership and want to spread what I have learned from you so far.

I want to bring pride to my nation, that's why I have decided to move on."

Robin listens to Victor, he knows Victor so well that he was aware that every feeling he has expressed, every word he has spoken is true. Victor continues,

"What do you suggest, and how do you feel about this Robin? "

Robin: "That's true Victor, I have always felt that a brother of mine is taking care of my business in my absence. These days I cannot imagine my business and success without you. Though I have created this company, it is you who took it to the top, to the heights where the closest competitor is way behind us. I feel that it will be a challenge to stay ahead of the competition without your wisdom and skills. It is the same company, but I know how entire organization has transformed under your leadership. Though you are young, you have earned respect at each level, from the janitor to the CEO. We could never have accomplished that without you.

I do not feel good about you leave us".

He stops for a while, and Victor asks, "What should I do then Robin? If that's the case, I will decline the offer".

Robin, "Victor, you have assessed your elder brother less. Your question had two parts. One, that how do I feel, and second, what do I suggest. I have answered one part, these are my feelings and my suggestion is not based on my feelings. Suggestions need to be far-sighted and logic driven.

I am feeling upset and emotional at this moment, which is because of the intensity of the topic we are discussing. You are a person with very high potential. To stop you is like to try to hold an ocean in a bucket, no wise person will do that. Even if one does that, it will not work.

I had known it that someday you would move as you have dreams and a will to achieve them. Do not think that it's me who has given you what you have today. I had hired many people in the organization, some at much higher positions from where you have started. I have not given you anything, you have earned everything with your strong qualities, so it is not a time for you or me to think illogically."

Even under emotions Robin manages his emotions well, this is the sign of a true leader.

"If I were you, I would have thought in a similar manner. When I need to grow, I have to go. Your missions are greater than average people, and I know that wherever you go, you will spread goodness. Let me tell you a story I heard from a friend,

Monk's Mysterious Ritual

Once a monk with his pupil went to a village, let us call it village A. The people in the village were very arrogant, no one bothered to ask them for water. Unrestrictedly, they mocked them, called them beggars. They stole their belongings, and someone even threw stones at them. They were humiliated in all possible ways. With such disgrace, they left the village.

On the way back, as a ritual, the monk had to bless the village. At the border of the village, he raised his hand toward the village and blessed, "May you all always remain settled here, and may all-sufficient resources be blessed to this village.. May you all be prosperous here and no calamity or paucity forces you to leave this village". With this, the monk and his pupil left the village.

On the way ahead, there was another village, we will call it Village B. The people residing in village B were kind, helpful and caring. They greeted them with flowers, served them with best fruits and the meal they had. They even made comfortable arrangements for them to sleep. This village was ideal, all people were good. They remained here for a few days and shared the words of wisdom with the villagers. Once they were ready to leave, the whole village gathered there for farewell and requested them to visit again. While they leave, the monk had to complete the ceremony of blessing the village. He raised his hands once again and consecrated, "May your village abandon, and you all move in different directions. May you stay away from this place and never come back. May God fulfill my blessing to you."

The pupil was confused that why monk gave good consecrations to people of village A and cursed village B where the people were so kind and helpful. His confusion reflected on his face.

Monk noticed the bewilderment on his pupil's face and asked, "My son, is there something which you are thinking and concerned about?"

The pupil queried, "Father, I am confused with your different benedictions to the villages. Your blessing to Village B sounds more of a curse.

Monk smiled and replied, "Son, there is a deep connotation to my sanctifications. Village A people were devilish, and wherever they go they will spread evil. If God confined them to one place, movements of evil would be restricted.

Whereas the people in village B were divine, they were helpful and kind. If they go out of the village, they will make this world a better place by virtue of their qualities."

Pupil now understood the hidden meaning in the monk's blessings.

Victor everyone who knows you has confidence that you will spread the magic of high standards and qualities. I would not like to hold you back, if I do that my decision would be against humanity and your growth."

Robin denotes richness not only at materialistic but also at spiritual levels, a lovely soul, Victor thinks while Robin continues,

"I will not stop you, contribute, exceed, and grow people and yourself. Life is a journey of accomplishing your ideas and creating a fortune.

Feel free to come back, my doors are always open for you."

Today is the first time in all these years that Robin has expressed his feelings explicitly. Sometimes we express feelings when we split ways.

"Leaders honor their spoken and unspoken words, they live by it."

The authority and flexibility Robin has given him depicts his unspoken feelings, he was truthful and honest inside out. Victor feels a pang inside, feels even more emotional. As Robin has just conveyed that decisions should not be dependent on emotions, he joysticks his emotions and further speaks,

"Robin, I appreciate the support you have always provided me. Our professional relation will take a different course in future, I need guidance from you.

As a word of advice, what would you like to tell me?"

Robin finishes his drink, he calls the waiter to order another one. He feels calm and relaxed now.

"The weight of pending decisions creates heaviness, to evacuate that heaviness we must decide."

Robin, "Sure Vick, I will be glad to guide you, but preceding to that I would like to make you clear on feelings and emotions. Usually people use these words interchangeably, they do not differentiate between them.

There also is no harm unless it spoils the message. When I talk about feelings, I mean what I feel in my heart, when I talk about emotions I talk about what is in my mind in an agitated state.

Confusing? The word emotion for me is the agitated state of mind. The word feeling for me is the calm state of mind. People generally do not differentiate between these, whenever I have doubt I ask about the specific meaning from the speaker, in what relation he has used the word.

To communicate effectively, the speaker and the audience, need to have the same vocabulary or meaning of the words, means they must know the precise context of the word. Otherwise, it results in total loss of message. That's why people interpret things differently. Remember, there are no right or wrong interpretations, there are interpretations only.

I will quote an example from my recent meeting on a government project. In the meeting, one of our partners stood up and told that they would use XTN for deployment of networks across the country. He had a very efficient, economical and detailed plan and he presented it very well to the officials. However the officials seemed unconvinced with what he proposed. I found his presentation striking and was trying to figure out why it is not making an impact. In the end, they concluded that despite the plan being notable they were not convinced on the company we had chosen, and hence, the proposal got rejected

It was a shock for both my partner and me. I could not hold my question, and asked them what was wrong with the company we had chosen for deployment. As per us, XTN was the best for this project, and we had done admirable work together in the past, they had always met or improved the cost, quality and time criteria.

One of the officials responded that they do not feel that XTN is the right vendor. To get the project plan approved, we need to change it to their authentic, tried and trusted partner Xoldin Company. My doubts helped us to win the project on the spot.

XTN, its full name is Xoldin Technology Networks Inc. It was the same company the government wanted for deployment, but they were not aware of its abbreviated form, which we had used in our presentation. They thought of it as some unknown company, which we hired to keep our costs low. We explained it to them and bagged the project.

On the way back my partner was laughing at how ignorant government officials were. I interrupted him and told that they were not ignorant, the term we had used was a stranger to them, and it was our responsibility to present the information in an easily understandable manner to them.

This is how different meaning of words can change the course of actions, it can move in entirely different directions.

The purpose of telling this incident is you should always understand the difference between words for example emotions, feelings and judgment.

The brain should always drive judgments. So when I make a decision that relates to you, I keep my feelings and emotions aside and do the right thing.

Your span of influence will further increase and you need to take care of these minor things.

You should always use the tool which applies."

Victor thinks, he actually does not differentiate between his feelings and emotions, and he has always thought that if a person is engaged he should be emotionally involved in work. But somehow it was the reason for some individuals to take it to their egos and damage internally and externally. Instead of doing the right things, they got emotionally involved in decision making and instead of making it a plan to work they made it a prestige issue. If someone challenged their idea, they felt offended, their emotions and feelings barred their brain from assessing the real value of ideas presented by others.

Though these things have not impacted him yet, Victor thinks that when he grows older, reaches the peak of his destiny, he might turn into a person who thinks he is always right.

An individual may not be right always, even if he has achieved the heights, the knowledge changes every day, business scenarios change, new technologies interrupt, and generations change. He needs to be open to the ideas of others and put the right ones to use.

Robin's words interrupt his thoughts.

"Shall we order the dinner Vick?"

Victor suggests, "I am not feeling hungry, but this is the right time so we can order."

Robin, "OK, let us order something, I am in a mood for hot and spicy food today."

Victor joked, "Shall we decide the food menu with feelings or brain?"

Robin snickers, "In a regular life, with your brain, but sometimes you should take liberty and have fun. You know health is wealth, but sometimes we should use that wealth."

They chortle together and call the waiter,

Robin, "Can you recommend something extra spicy, which lowers my risk of heart attack and stroke?"

Waiter recommends a few items from the menu.

Victor exclaims, "Wow, what a contradictory order, you want to eat spicy and decrease chances of illness at the same time."

Robin, "Of course both can be done at the same time. Food is a tool to keep you in healthy shape. Right spicy foods actually have the qualities to reduce your risks of cardiac disease."

They discuss food now, the heaviness had disappeared totally. A waiter serves them food. Robin continues,

"Like good thoughts and ideas are food for the brain, we need to consume right food to stay energetic and fit. Sometimes people become uncompetitive because they lack energy levels.

This body is a gift from God, and we must take essential care of it. Good food habits are a specific subject to discuss, many books exist on this subject.

An average person does not develop healthy eating habits, so typically he spends the first half of his life to earn wealth and the second half, to spend it on medical bills.

To maintain good health takes lesser efforts, but once you have a health disorder, it's hard to recover and sometimes impossible.

A healthy lifestyle with healthy food habits is the key to live strong.

It is a habit you must develop Victor."

Though Victor exercises and meditates, he has not paid much attention to his eating habits. He engrosses in work and misses timely food. The body is also equally important like thoughts, ideas, and actions.

He decides to study this subject more to stay healthy throughout life.

Chapter – 14

"Advice for Life"

The Vampire of Bragging on Past Success

"Past learnings become obsolete with time, you need to learn every day. You must learn from different cultures, concepts, ideas and experiences. This learning advances your life toward meaningful achievement & contribution for greater benefits."

Robin and Victor finish their dinner, and Robin offers to drop him at his home which is around two hours distance from the hotel. "So now, I will come on 'Advice for Life' Vick" and it will give you a kick.

"There is so much to learn from you Robin, I would miss your company."

"There is nothing like to miss someone these days, just pick your phone or drop me an email."

"I will share with you what I have learned as an entrepreneur and in my life."

Life is full of highs and lows, and we need to acknowledge that as part and parcel of life. It has positives and negatives too, sometimes my business has gone through depressions, but I never lost hope. I had confidence in my mission, and I always looked at the positive side. Darkness does not end darkness, it takes light to end darkness. In a similar way I knew that thinking about negatives would not help me, I worked hard."

"Throughout my journey I got exposed to a lot of things, and I would like to summarize those things to help you further.

Most of your values are already clear. I consider six concepts crucial, which I have learned through my global travels, business, and personal experiences.

<u>Control your Sins:</u>

There are seven deadly sins defined as pride, greed, extravagance, envy, gluttony, wrath, and sloth.

You should always control your vices otherwise, they will command you. Pride here is arrogance, which hurts other humans. Do not misunderstand it with the right pride which you earn with superior work. Rest of the sins are pretty damaging and can turn you into a monster. The people who are not able to control their vices meet a tragic end.

I had a very efficient employee who got into the habit of excessive drinking. Under the influence of alcohol he beat his wife and kids, and one day they left him and never looked back. This culminated gloominess and depression and he ended his life, he hanged himself.

People carry on with these sins until they get punishments, you must not do that. You should control because that is the correct deed. If you follow the right path, you remain blessed till eternity.

This lesson is fundamental, which you must follow to be God's favorite child.

I know Victor, you do not have any of these sins. But when you become powerful, the 'Vampire of Sins' tries to overtake you and let you down. They are spread across the globe uniformly looking for a weak prey, ones who they can easily target.

You need to be mindful that you keep them away from your life."

Victor, "Robin, do you also feel that vampires of sins might attack you as you are powerful and successful".

Robin, "Yes Victor, they try to attack me every day, I find a lot of opportunities where those vampires can bite me. But I know what the end results will be and decline to give in, remember 'Headline Test'. If you have the vision to see and realize the deadly consequences of the sins, you will never allow them to attack you".

Victor, "Thanks Robin, this is a priceless insight, and I will take care of it. What is the second concept?"

Understand Cultural and semantic differences:

When I traveled across the globe, I found that we must understand the cultural differences. In some countries, you are not allowed to wear shorts in public places, people have different religious faiths, and in some cases due to the economic environment, the way of thinking is different.

Some cultures trust and some are cautious. Study cultures of the countries before you visit in order not to look odd there. There are cultures where people meet and greet differently, especially with women you need to be very appropriate in greeting manners.

Here, we do hug occasionally, some cultures consider it very bad. So every country is different. We know the rules of our country and are habitual of living them, still sometimes we unknowingly make mistakes. You need to understand the semantic difference as well which means the countries can have different meanings for words, phrases, signs, and symbols—and what they stand for, their significance in those cultures.

A sign of positivity here can be a sign of vulgarity in some cultures, so educate yourself beforehand.

As you might not be able to learn all the things at one go, the best approach would be to observe before you act. You know that a lot of knowledge has spread around us, we need to learn from it.

A kid learns to walk and talk, simply by the power of observation and practice. This act is what you have to do, you need to be a kid, and you need to have an observation ability of a child. But remember here, kids are kids, they can fall cry and stand again.

If you make mistakes, you do not get the treatment as a kid, and the impression or perception which you will leave on people will stay with them, many years after you have left them. Average people judge others by perception, which might be totally away from reality. However perception is a reality today. People do not buy the right products, they buy the products which they perceive as best. That is simple human psychology, you need not be a rocket scientist to understand this.

Victor, I have faced this once, people perceived me wrongly, and I think they still carry the same perception, but might be it was my fault. Faults remain as faults and leave the same impact even if done in ignorance."

Robin, continues, "You are unknown to the people and the place. Do not assess yourself on the qualities which you have, those qualities might be excellent but only individuals who know you well will value those.

However, in a new environment, people will not know you so they will put you on the scale of perception and evaluate. If you leave even one wrong impression, it will become manifold - multiplied by the number of people who get to know about it.

Hope you find it helpful Victor, and not getting bored."

"Of course Robin I enjoyed it, a very useful advice, a lot of people are affected by the bad perception others carry for them. I have an experience as well. Once I heard bad feedback about a person, and avoided him. However when I got a chance to meet him over some issue, I got to know that he is a fantastic guy.

People did not look at his right qualities and rated his honesty as arrogance. So, I put him in compliance function, and the performance there improved drastically.

If I had not got an opportunity to meet him, I would have still carried the same perception, and he might have lost his job.

Even as a kid, most of the people perceived me as a weak child, they always teased me and never took any action beyond that.

It was only my sister who envisaged me differently and used to tell me that I will do uncommonly in life."

"When I remember those days, I feel great about my sister who with her own efforts, kept a ray of hope lightened. I truly love her," revisits Victor.

"Yes Victor, you were lucky to have a sister like that, who inspired, cared and sowed the seeds of hope in you.

I actually had no one, but I still succeeded, God was on my side".

"These are the things you need to take care of, now I will share the concepts which will help you to accelerate

Partnership First:

Always work with the spirit of partnership, you will need many collaborations to grow the business. To select a right partner becomes essential here, once a partner has passed the criteria, trust them that they would do a good job. When you trust, do it with open eyes.

Mutual trust and honesty are essential for any successful partnership. Remember, word partnership begins with part, you need to be part of each other. It's crucial that all parts work in tandem to produce desired outcomes.

You need to respect, work and play on the strength of your partners. If you take examples of successful companies, they believe in partnership. The market reach of all products is a result of various successful partnerships.

This union makes a product successful, as no one has the hundred percent capability to produce the best. However when you enter into a partnership, you can harness on the strength of each partner.

You also need to ensure that all partners are respected and collaborate fairly.

We also won major deals with the right combination of our partners". After the concept of partnership first, Robin takes a pause.

"I caught it Robin, as superlative teamwork works at a functional level, the partnership is an essential element of success on larger platforms.

I will always keep in mind the need to develop a true partnership, to make each one of us succeed. It is no more about individual success but, collective success".

"That's correct Victor, no more individuality, it's more about common goals of the partnership. Remember even more when you get married." They chuckle.

"Next point is innovation:

Innovate:

Inventions are the top of the list, however, innovation is the second best. As Steve Jobs enunciated, *"Japan's very interesting. Some people think it copies things. I do not think that anymore. I think what they do is reinvent things. They will get something that's already been invented and study it until they thoroughly understand it. In some cases, they understand it better than the original   inventor."*

Systems, processes, products and services of the company exist previous to you join it, you need to see what can be done to improve and make these more user-friendly and easy to use.

The simple user experience of the most complex things will make your products more successful.

Companies which do not keep customers in mind when they design their products become non-existent sooner or later.

Remember that we exist because our products exist, products exist because the demand exists, and demand exists because customer exists. Always keep it as a foundation of your strategy that it is the customer who ultimately buys your product and makes your company profitable. And everyone excluding you is your customer, one slip and they go.

They might always give you exceptional requirements, sometimes even unrealistic. The customer can be incorrect but he is the king, and his wish should be your command. If not perfect, always attempt to deliver the closest possible product.

Introduce your product and keep innovating, one day it will achieve perfection and meet the requirements which once we thought were impossible.

We can count the original inventions which turned around the existence of mankind, but innovations converted it into millions of products and the process is ceaseless.

Innovation improves the quality of life. Innovation is not limited only to tangible products, you can innovate everything which exists. Products, services, tools, home, style and almost everything.

You can even innovate your sentences, instead of saying, "Do not worry, I will handle problems" say "Rest assured, solutions are there."

Where you had two negative words in the first sentence 'Do not' and 'Worry', which will give a background impression of 'not and worry.' When you innovate your sentence, these got replaced by 'assurance and solutions'. Feel the impact and make continuous changes.

Innovate, innovate and just innovate.

Use, scrap and recycle Learnings:

Always recycle your learnings, see that what in your knowledge can be utilized, discarded or recycled.

This process will create additional space which will help you to learn more. Success is to use and keep the applicable knowledge and discard useless stuff.

Change is necessary for any individual or corporate success. With the use of timeworn knowledge, the chances of getting dull and weary are high. Inelasticity is like a slow poison, which ultimately triggers death. Use, scrap and recycle mix it with acquiring new skills, you will keep you and your organization full of relevance and vitality.

There are disruptive information and technology changes that make the world shine and revolve by its virtues. Alvin Toffler understood and phrased this requirement beautifully by saying, "The illiterate of the 21st Century will not be those who cannot read or write, but those who cannot learn, unlearn and relearn."

Change Adaptability is the key to success. Learn daily, edit your learnings daily to remove the unrequired information.

Take a break and have fun:

You must always remember that even machines need a break and maintenance. As a human, it is important to take breaks from your routine life and have fun, it helps to regain and reenergize yourself. Breaks are the times which you spend with your friends and families. It can be used to celebrate your success or do retrospection or introspection.

After all, you have gained so much and paid

special attention to routine tasks throughout the year, you deserve breaks too.

Rejuvenate, reenergize and recreate yourself during these breaks.

So Victor, these are my six cents to you, advice for life. Mix it with the concepts which you have learned and you will never face a crisis in your life."

Victor thanks Robin for his advice and then they discuss his replacement as the show must go on.

Victor, "Robin, I have someone in mind, he has mentored me since I was a zero. I am sure that he is better than me."

"Victor, there is no comparison, every individual is unique, and that individuality must be respected. God does not create replicas, one creation only once."

Victor justifies, "I understand it Robin, what I meant is that this individual is very competitive, already working in a leadership role, has the required skills, and moreover he is great a human being.

To me, he appears to be the right fit for replacement. His name is Patrick."

Robin, "As we need to close this position before you leave. I depend on you to hire the right candidate, remember that you have already set exceptional standards which would be challenging for anyone to maintain."

Victor, "Yes Robin, rest assured we will get the right person to do the job."

Next couple of weeks goes to interview candidates for replacement. Patrick scores on top of all, so he gets the role.

After Robin meets Patrick, he also gets reassurance that Victor's legacy will sustain under the new leader.

It is Victor's last day in office, and there is a grand farewell, people have tears in their eyes to see him leave.

"I will be available for all of you to provide necessary guidance and support, whether the matter is personal or professional. I am merely a phone call away, please feel free to contact whenever you need me".

With these words, he departs.

Victor's overseas success:

Victor continues to live up to the concepts. He created new dimensions to do business, initially he was head of one region. Most of the corporates divide the world into three regions – APAC (Asia Pacific), EMEA (Europe, the Middle East, and Africa) and AMS (Americas).

He starts afresh, observes people for a couple of months and acquires an understanding of operating business models. With high standards of delivery and successful partnerships, he breaks major deals in Asia.

His name gains credibility worldwide and in a couple of years, he becomes a mentor to hundreds of people.

The company values his contribution, and they want him to lead at a worldwide level. He is now thirty-six and has never let the vampires to success overtake him.

He closes his memoir takes a deep breath, looks outside the window again, his face radiates when he says,

"This is just a beginning."

A Request:

It takes only one minute, if you have liked Vampires to Success and you will like it to reach masses, please post a review, your reviews will make a difference.

Below is the link:

https://www.amazon.com/Vampires-Success-journey-Accomplishing-Creating-ebook/dp/B01FPSJS3G

Other Books by VJ Cartier:

❖ **Narendra Modi 7 Life Lessons: A Lion Among The Leaders (India Series Book 1)**

   https://www.amazon.com/dp/B01M0CIK3W

❖ **Ramdev Baba 7 Life Lessons: From A Village Lad To Yog And Biz Guru (India Series Book 2)**

   https://www.amazon.com/dp/B01MPWN68R

❖ **THINK DEEP ACT WISE: 5 Steps to Make Your Relations Work For You**

   https://www.amazon.com/dp/B01LXREDGA

❖ **Swallow That Shark: 51 Irrefutable Laws to Accelerate Your Life**

   https://www.amazon.com/dp/B01N0GU48D